For Kit
      in memory
of our son Scott
& daughter Danny
Thanks for your
encouragement
           Richard

Unsafe at
Any Altitude

Unsafe at Any Altitude

Richard Francis Schaden
with Chris Moore

Copyright © 2021 by Richard Francis Schaden.

Library of Congress Control Number: 2021906973
ISBN: Hardcover   978-1-6641-6705-6
              Softcover   978-1-6641-6704-9
              eBook   978-1-6641-6703-2

All rights reserved. No part of this book may be reproduced or transmitted in any form or by any means, electronic or mechanical, including photocopying, recording, or by any information storage and retrieval system, without permission in writing from the copyright owner.

Print information available on the last page.

Rev. date: 08/12/2021

To order additional copies of this book, contact:
Xlibris
844-714-8691
www.Xlibris.com
Orders@Xlibris.com
824950

Contents

Preface 1
Prologue 3
Chapter 1   Flight Test – *The experiential path to engineering in the courtroom* 11
Chapter 2   Wolverine Air Charter – *A law firm is started* 26
Chapter 3   Schifko – *Learning the legal process from criminal law to airplane products* 31
Chapter 4   Cessna's Flat Spin – *Finally, an airplane design case* 48
Chapter 5   The Rio Negro – *The NTSB and challenging the published cause of an airplane crash* 63
Chapter 6   Piston Twins – *Challenging historical airplane design concepts* 77
Chapter 7   Kenneally – *There's a whole lot of shakin' going on* 98
Chapter 8   Learjet – *A bad design notwithstanding, can become very popular* 106
Chapter 9   Northwest Airlines Flight 255 – *Warnings can correct pilot error* 127
Chapter 10 United Airlines Flight 811 – *Aging Aircraft* 141
Chapter 11 United Airlines Flight 232 – *A single failure should not cause loss of an airliner and passengers* 154
Chapter 12 Flight Without a Fin – *A great stretch to blame the pilot* 168
Chapter 13 TWA Airlines Flight 800 – *Anything to save a brand* ... 185

Chapter 14 Tail Power and the Boeing 737 - *It wagged its tail and rolled over* 202

Chapter 15 The Boeing MAX and Longitudinal Stability - *An economic decision leads to the loss of many lives*..221

Epilogue..243

Preface

Upon opening, you might find this book appears to be my autobiography. But I see myself as the messenger or vehicle that carries the story, starting with experiential learning, a concept that had become a way of life, juxtaposed next to academia and formal training.

This is a story about crossing the disciplines of engineering and law to create safer transportation, ultimately, more specifically in the sky. Product liability law helps force engineering design to truly serve the needs of man.

Formally, I was educated as an aeronautical engineer, airplane pilot, and next a lawyer.

It would seem to an outsider that these are pretty complicated disciplines to mix. Yet from flight level 410, that is, 41,000 feet, metaphorically, standing away from the nitty-gritty details, it all integrates quite well.

All of law can be summarized as having three basic elements plus one important umbrella: (1) a person's duty to do no harm to another and act reasonably under the circumstances, of which failure to comply is referred to as committing a tort; (2) a person's duty to follow the rules of law, of which failure to comply is referred to as a crime; and (3) people's promises to do something such as transfer

1

property, provide a service, or complete some other transaction which are referred to as contracts.

All three of these should be under an umbrella of fairness. That is, don't ask for remedies to which you are not entitled, or you could say, don't go to court with dirty hands.

Now let's look at engineering. I believe that it is fair to define good engineering as the task of designing and constructing items to safely and effectively serve the needs of humankind, of which failure to comply is poor engineering. This concept fits nicely juxtaposed to the above basic concepts of law.

Airbags, collapsible steering wheels, padded dashboards, seat belts, and shoulder harnesses were not the result of engineering by the auto companies, but were the result of product liability lawsuits. It could be said that these items were engineered in the courthouse. Law has saved a lot of lives.

The courtroom has proven to be a great forum for evaluating design and an effective way to force change for safety.

Exculpatory: In this story, some names are real, and some are made up for reasons that may be obvious. Some facts are real, and others are just different as seen through the lens of different people or as remembered differently. Notwithstanding, the science and technology is accurate, although even in science there exist axioms, theories, and opinion.

Prologue

It was a cold February day in the early 1970s. I was climbing out of the Detroit City Airport in a small single-engine airplane, my dad to my right in the co-pilot's seat. This was his first time in an airplane of any kind. He was excited.

Gaining altitude over the cemetery at the departure end of the runway, we then passed over the tall brick and concrete buildings not far below and too close for comfort. But at this altitude, I was happy to get a glimpse of the Detroit River three miles in the distance. In case of trouble (engine failure, say), we could head for the water and hope for the best.

In those days, engine reliability was more of an issue, and engine-failure accidents were more common than I wanted to admit. Obviously, I didn't let my father know. It was also probably best he didn't fully understand the mission we were on.

I was headed to look at the wreckage of a single-engine Beechcraft airplane that had crashed in a field about sixty miles north of Detroit. It was a fatal crash that had killed the sole occupant, namely, the pilot. The family of the deceased had hired me as their lawyer. The only reason I think they hired me was that I was the only attorney with an office at the airport, a habit I still keep. My office was on the second floor of the terminal building. The door read Air Charter. Just below that hung another sign. "Honest lawyer, I win some of my cases," it said (the last part added by a couple of friends as a joke).

The case that I was setting out to investigate was likely one that no real lawyer would have been interested in pursuing. I wasn't even sure that I could help my clients. But as a young engineer and pilot, I hoped I could find something in the wreckage that would support the cause being something other than "pilot error." I knew, for instance, that the National Transportation Safety Board (NTSB) in their preliminary report had stated that "the engine had quit, which resulted in the pilot's fatal attempt at an off-airport 'engine out' landing." In this case, the "off-airport" landing took place in a field. What they hadn't stated was why the engine quit. I was hoping I could find out.

I was only a few years out of night law school at this point and had been cutting my teeth on criminal cases assigned to me by Wayne County's criminal court. I represented indigent clients who couldn't afford a lawyer. Two of those had been first-degree murder cases. Not exactly what I had been looking for when I left Boeing as an aeronautical engineer. But what could I expect? I had never worked for a law firm, never been a law clerk; I don't even think I had set foot in a courthouse before I left law school. Incidentally, I was handling my first cases before I passed the bar. I had been sworn in, as they called it, by a judge during the Detroit riots since there weren't enough lawyers to defend the hundreds charged with riot-related crimes. I learned a lot about the legal process this way; it was trial by fire. For a while, I would tell juries to bear with me, that this was my first felony case or first big case or first experience in this court, etc. I was looking for some empathy.

"I want to ask you," I would say to the jury, "not to hold my inexperience against my client." I'd finish the speech by adding,

"You'll find it out sooner or later, so I may as well say it now: I was educated as an engineer, so I'm not very good at spelling. I feel like Mark Twain when he said, 'I have no respect for a man that can only spell a word one way.'"

In the early 1970s, product liability claims were still relatively new, and precedent was developing rapidly. Claims against manufacturers were based on theories of negligence and warranty of "fitness for purpose," but with my background, I was more interested in putting the product's design on trial, which I was beginning to see had so often been the real cause behind an accident, and no one seemed to be focusing on this aspect.

With the Beechcraft crash, I didn't know what I was looking for or even if there was anything to find. However, since I was so new to these kinds of cases, and with my background working in Boeing's flight test department, I thought the only way I could become comfortable was to get as close as possible to that plane and ponder its last moments—getting my own eyes and hands on the hardware and the environment is a tactic that's served me well ever since.

After reaching the river, I leveled off at three thousand feet and pointed the little airplane northwest toward the accident site. God, I love to fly.

The NTSB had finished their investigation only days prior and removed the yellow ribbon securing the wreckage, but for the moment, they had left the plane lying in the field. It seemed to me I had a pretty short window to take a look.

Approaching the area, I descended to a lower altitude. My dad spotted the wreckage first and pointed to it. I then made several low passes over the area and decided the icy field was not a friendly place to land; however, the road on the other side of the fence running north and south looked pretty good. I landed there. Climbing from the cockpit, I put a few rocks under the wheels to keep the plane from rolling away while we took a look. We then climbed over the split-rail fence and hiked out to the wrecked airplane.

Although Dad seemed anxious to help in any way and was happy to fly with me, I doubt if he gave a thought toward the lawsuit likely to come from this mission. He certainly didn't know the result would be a loss paid by an insurance company he represented as an independent agent, and certainly, he didn't realize that the case would be tried in the Wayne County Circuit Court against one of his best friends, a lawyer from the usher's club at our church. He might have thought twice about coming, if he had.

We approached the crinkled, tangled mess of aluminum. Our first observation was that the plane had come down hard. It was also obvious from the propeller that the engine was not running at the time of impact. That was at least consistent with the NTSB's preliminary report.

My dad and I walked around the wreck and looked over the furrows it had made in the soil. I then caught him looking down the wreckage trail and up to the sky in the direction from which the plane had come, obviously tracing its path. I followed his eyes and looked over to my own plane parked in the road. With the Beechcraft before us, it was hard not to think about what it would be like to crash, something that I would learn only once in my life, at least to this point.

From there, I made my way to the engine compartment, hoping to spot anything obvious that could have contributed to its failure. Seeing nothing of note, I moved to the cockpit. There, I entered through the mangled door and under the jumble of overhead wires, tattered weather-stripping upholstery, and foam and settled into the rather broken pilot's seat. Gazing around the instrument panel, the gauges, toggles, etc., I tried to imagine what the pilot must have been going through in the final moments of the flight.

As a test engineer, and now with an office at the airport, I had seen my share of plane crashes. But up until now, I had never been inside the cockpit of a wreck after a fatal one; there was something strange and solemn about being here. The cabin was eerily quiet.

I got beyond the odd sense I felt and continued looking. After inspecting the gauges and placing my hand on the throttle, I looked below the instrument panel by my feet to the rudder pedals. There I saw a shoe. At closer look, the stump of the pilot's foot was still inside.

I nearly jumped out of the cockpit.

"You ok in there?" my dad asked.

"Yeah, I think I'm done here," I said and began to leave, but as I was about to get up, I noticed that the fuel selector valve was in the "off" position.

Interesting, I thought.

NTSB investigators had a strict policy not to move any of the controls. Had someone then done it after the official investigators left? As far as I could tell, I was the only person to climb into this twisted wreck. So why was the fuel selector valve in the "off" position?

Had the pilot done it? Did he make a mistake, or was it something else? It seemed to me that I had encountered something about this issue before. I recalled some confusion about this very handle.

"I thought you were climbing out," I heard my father say.

"I think I found something."

By this time in my flying life, I had been up in a lot of single-engine planes. I used to hang around the airport, carrying luggage and sweeping hangars just to get a chance to fly. Since I had earned various pilot's licenses, I had done whatever I could, if not to fly every plane, then at the very least to sit inside the cockpit to get a feel for how it was laid out.

I had seen this fuel selector valve before, and I knew it was installed in more than one type of airplane. Both the Piper Cherokee series and the Beech used the same valve handle. However, though it was the same handle, casting, and shape, one airplane manufacturer used the handle end of the casting as the pointer, while the other used the opposite end. According to the pilot's family, he had flown several other single-engine airplanes, which made me think he might have gotten used to the reverse orientation of the handle.

I was also aware of a recent government report titled "Design-Induced Pilot Error," which had been on my desk in the office for some time. One of its chapters detailed accidents where the pilot had mispositioned the fuel selector valve, based on design, and had inadvertently shut off the fuel when the intention was to select another tank. I had no notion of this when I flew out to the wreck, but now the report came to mind.

The shutoff valve in question had three toggle positions: Left Tank, Right Tank, and Off. A pilot, reading the indicator backward, could easily switch the tank to Off in an attempt to switch from the near-empty tank to the full one. The plane would then continue flying on the fuel trapped in the system until it ran out, which could take several minutes before his engine would fail. He'd be losing altitude then, and while time was running out, he'd be confused about why the engine had stopped. He would be thinking he was on a full fuel tank. Even if he discovered the error, he would still need twenty or thirty seconds just to get the engine to fire again. That's if he ever did discover it.

I took another look at the valve and thought, *we have a case, a design case.*

On the short flight back to Detroit City Airport, my dad and I talked a little about the crash, but he seemed uneasy with the topic, and we largely didn't speak. I spent the time thinking about fatal crashes I had known. Very early on, I had a sense at how destructive they could be. It started when I was a young boy in Detroit and a British military plane had crashed in our neighborhood, killing the crew and everyone inside the house in a terrible fire. And flying out of Detroit City Airport on a weekly basis and hanging out with hangar bums, I became aware of a fatal crash every couple of months. Wrecks, injuries, and death were a way of life for pilots in those early days. We had the idea that flying was inherently dangerous and that you accepted those risks if you had been bitten by the flying bug, but I was coming to believe that many of these disasters could have been avoided but for one single defect in design. I had come across similar flaws on the drawing boards when I worked as an engineer both at Boeing and Continental Aviation and Engineering. But it had never clicked for me before how much safer planes could be.

On that day in February, however, I found not only a case for my client but also a lifelong mission.

CHAPTER 1

Flight Test

Somebody said that it couldn't be done
But he with a chuckle replied
That "maybe it couldn't," but he would be one
Who wouldn't say so till he'd tried.

—Edgar Guest

Outdoor Laboratory

I remember being cold a lot of the time. The old farmer had retrieved me from my house in Detroit to take me to the old family farm on the Rideau Lakes near Westport, Ontario, up in Canada. I sat for two days, including one night, in a rocking chair tied to the bed of his pickup.

You'd go to jail for a thing like that today, but at the time, I don't remember thinking there was anything wrong with it; neither did anyone else. Of course, we traveled the old truck routes, so our top speed was low compared to today's highway speeds.

It was late June 1953. I remember that because Queen Elizabeth had recently been coronated. She was twenty-seven at the time. I was fifteen and a long way from royalty, but I wouldn't exchange those summers for anything. That farm was a self-contained world full of machines of varying complexity, and I had a role in keeping it all going. The Sears, Roebuck & Company catalogue became like a close friend as I ordered what was needed to keep the machines in working order, such as horse-drawn mowers, cutters, rakes, and binders. I also repaired the horse harnesses, attachments, and buckles.

More often than not, the Lower Rideau Lake was the place I chose to explore. However, I never imagined that in the course of my explorations, I would make a discovery that would help shape the course I'd take in life.

The boat I was rowing that early summer day was among a small fleet of flat-bottom rowboats made on the farm of white pine, cut and milled from the land for that purpose. These boats leaked like sieves when we first put them in the water (my first lesson in the concept of diffusivity pertinent to fluids and solids); soon the planks swelled, and the boats sealed themselves. We built them for the renters who came and stayed in the cabins on the lakeshore in the summer months.

That day, I rowed to a nearby cove. On the bottom, I spotted something silver and angular partially hidden in the sand ten feet below.

I leaped into the water and swam to the bottom, eyes open, without a mask. I could see that it was an old-fashioned outboard motor. It had the name "Thor" embossed on the fuel tank. I had heard of Thor washing machine motors but never knew that they made outboards. It had only one cylinder and said one-horsepower on the side. I tied a rope to the outboard and returned to the surface.

I pulled the one-horsepower Thor motor back to the barn in the horse-drawn wagon that I had been using for transportation. Since the land was steep and uneven and the tractors tended to get stuck, all the farm equipment was pulled by horses. They broke down a lot less frequently and required only feed that grew on the land.

After I figured out how to pull the flywheel, I learned how a magneto worked. I found from the manual, ordered from the Sears catalogue, that there was a magnet in the flywheel; the spinning flywheel created electrical energy, which was stored in a capacitor, which could be discharged and make a spark. The spark in turn ignited the fuel in the cylinder, driving the piston down, which spun the propeller that drove the boat. Unknown to me, I was learning something about the first two branches of basic physics: mechanics and electricity.

The first time I took it out in the lake, it stalled near the middle, and I needed to row back to the dock. But by August, I had the motor running and managed to take my first trip to Westport—population 600—on the other side of the lake. I was disappointed to discover what little there was to do. But I was never disappointed in rebuilding that motor or working on any of the machines on the farm where I could get my hands dirty and learn outside of a classroom.

It set me on a path that led to the Boeing Airplane Company right out of engineering school, an opportunity that saw me not only at the drawing board and going up in test flights, but also investigating plane crashes and getting my hands dirty.

American Airlines Flight 1

A year into my job at Boeing, I was assigned to help investigate at the crash site of American Airlines Flight 1, which had killed ninety-five people in Queens, New York. At the time, it was the greatest loss of life in American aviation history. Several wealthy and well-known people were on board. One victim was a friend of President Eisenhower. The crash occurred in less than a foot of water in the Pumpkin Patch Channel of Jamaica Bay. It was March 1, 1962.

At that point, I had been working at Boeing under a year, having started with the company in the summer of 1961 right out of the University of Detroit's aeronautical engineering program. Seven of us had driven across the country in separate cars from Michigan. I had a '59 Chevy convertible. The others drove sports cars: MGs, Triumphs, and an Austin-Healey.

Up until the crash of Flight 1, I had been stuck behind a desk and drawing board in the engineering department in Seattle, which I was growing tired of. At least now I was able to get out of the office and get my hands dirty even though it was a bit eerie on the swampy ground where almost a hundred people died.

In Jamaica Bay, I mainly walked around in muck boots with a five-gallon bucket and pulled pieces of the aircraft off the bottom. The largest we found was about the size of a small automobile.

Flight 1 went down just minutes after takeoff from Idlewild Airport, now JFK, on a nonstop for Los Angeles. At about 1,600 feet, the plane began uncontrollably rolling left and right and wagging its tail (known as a Dutch roll), until it finally entered a near-vertical dive and crashed into brackish marshland at about a seventy-degree angle. Later that year, the Civil Aeronautics Board (CAB) determined the crash had been caused by a short circuit in the automatic pilot system caused by a one-time manufacturing error.

We flew back to Seattle on a United Airlines DC-6, a four-engine propeller aircraft, with a stop at Chicago's Midway Airport. On this long flight home, I pondered the possible causes of the crash of our 707. Based on the various ground witnesses' description of the plane's gyrations after takeoff, I was thinking of "Dutch roll." Dutch roll had started to be a plague that began when the swept-wing transports arrived on the scene.

Months later, when I read the CAB's report, I was curious of their insignificant attention to the Dutch roll issue. Yes, an errant autopilot input may have been the trigger, but too little attention was given to this unstable maneuver.

I didn't spend much time studying the crash of American Airlines Flight 1. I was filling a role for the company, but the event helped me form an opinion about plane crashes and apparent lack of objectivity of government investigations that I wouldn't soon forget. My takeaway was that Boeing and the insurance companies had a little too much influence in the crash investigations and the published cause. While my opinion was still that of a journeyman engineer, I believed that the stated cause of the crash technically missed the mark.

I had already spent ten months in Boeing's engineering building in Renton, Washington, where I worked in the aerodynamic section, responsible for airplane performance and stability and control. I had also done a co-op period during engineering school at the school's wind tunnel and had earned various pilot licenses when I was in Detroit.

My dream was never to be stuck flying a desk or drawing board.

Now back from the crash in New York, it seemed like I was trapped inside the offices with a thousand engineers and their helpers swirling around like clones of one another; there was gray metal as far as I could see and no windows in sight. The atmosphere was bleak and depressing. I wanted to see the sky, and more than anything, I wanted to play with the airplanes.

Flight Test

An opportunity came out of the blue, so to speak. While I loved flying and wanted to fly airplanes and explore maneuvers and performance, I spent any free time I had either in flying club light airplanes or down on the docks on Lake Washington. Sometimes, when sailboat owners would find themselves short of crew, they'd recruit people to perform certain tasks on the water or to act as ballast.

On one occasion, I was asked to join the crew of a fifty-foot sailing sloop to man the jib sheets. As it turned out, the owner was the chief of Boeing flight test, Bill Lieberman. I couldn't believe my luck.

I took the chance and explained that I was working in the engineering department but that I really wanted to move into flight test. "I'm a pilot," I said. "I don't want to be stuck behind a desk for much longer."

Surprisingly, he told me to come to his office on Monday morning, which I did. Before I knew it, I was working in Boeing's flight test department as a flight test engineer. This department was legendary at the time.

Now I should explain that there was a big difference between a flight test engineer, which was my job, and a test pilot. The test pilots weren't shy of reminding us of the difference. They were aces, hotshots, top guns, and acted like it. They also seemed to think they ran the place, which was not far from the truth in those days.

Around the test hangar, there was a story of a famous test pilot, Tex Johnston, who took an early Boeing 707 and flew it inverted over Lake Washington during a hydroplane race on a Sunday afternoon. Since he assumed no one would believe what they had just seen, he turned the plane around and did it again. He claims he knew the 707 was capable of doing such a maneuver without harm to the aircraft. I had my doubts. But that was the type of personality you would encounter among many of the test pilots then.

Even though I was never one of the Tex Johnstons at Boeing, I still got to get out of the office and up in the sky. Aside from playing with the aircraft, there were other perks as well, like every member of the team was able to go "weightless" at least once on the Boeing transports just to get the feel of it. The plane would fly a parabolic arc, and the centrifugal force at the top of its arc offsets gravity for a time, and the passengers go weightless. These flights were nicknamed a flight in the "vomit comet." Such flights were also used to train astronauts for zero gravity.

There were some hazards during test flights, but most of it was routine. We planned for failures; after all, we created them and recorded the results.

There was never a fatal crash while I was there. However, there was a fatal crash of a 707 a couple of years before I arrived, so we were aware that it could happen, which made our preparation all the more thorough.

My first flight test project was in Seattle, flying out of Boeing Field as part of a team to evaluate the use of a new turbo-fan jet engine, known as the JT8D, being developed then for use on a new design, which would come to be known as the Boeing 727. The test bed for the flights was the old prototype for the B707, which was Boeing's first commercial jetliner. The prototype was known as the 367-80. Today, that aircraft sits in the Smithsonian Air and Space Museum in Washington, D.C.

I was primarily involved in aerodynamics and instrumentation. We designed sensors that measured flight data for post-flight analysis. The sensors were often referred to as transducers in those days. The devices would take a mechanical input, such as force or pressure, and create an electronic signal in order to record data. This experience would help me greatly much later down the line when I was presenting safer design alternatives in the courtroom.

After the JT8D project, we worked mostly on certification testing for several other new models. We would demonstrate compliance with the Federal Aviation Administration's (FAA) design and performance regulations. Part of the certification testing we underwent for the FAA called for us to simulate a cabin failure and decompression at high altitude. For that purpose, we rigged a window in the cabin of a B720B to intentionally blow out at high altitude to experience rapid decompression. The first test was more than exciting. The noise was deafening; the temperature dropped to about minus forty degrees, and the instruments were covered in ice fog. Fortunately, we had already undergone tests on the ground to see how we would respond at very high altitudes with low oxygen. My recollection was that at cruising altitudes without oxygen, I was good for about eight seconds of clear consciousness. Thus, I was somewhat prepared for what happened in the sky.

Najeeb Halaby was the head of the FAA at that time. That made him the man we all wanted to please. We would often joke, "Our father who art in Washington, Halaby be his name." His daughter Lisa ended up marrying King Hussein of Jordan and became Queen Noor. Apparently, she had met the king, who was a pilot, while he was visiting Boeing to shop for airliners for his country's flag carrier.

Wichita and Learjet

In the spring of 1962, I was sent to Wichita, Kansas. My assignment was twofold: to attend engineering graduate school at Wichita State University at the company's request and to work on flight testing the latest version of the Air Force's B52 bomber. Flight testing this eight-engine airplane was a great learning experience. The B52 was a strong platform and a sound aircraft. We often joked when we had an engine flameout that we were faced with the dreaded seven-engine approach and landing.

I did notice that designing and building for the military didn't seem to have the same marketing and economic influence as the commercial business.

At the base in Wichita, I was asked to work on aircraft structural issues rather than aerodynamic and fluid mechanics, which had previously been my focus. We installed more than five hundred strain gauges and sensors on one of the B52H test aircraft to collect the stress and strain data on the airframe. First, we recorded and analyzed structural dynamic behavior to make sure that we weren't creating dynamic oscillations and/or vibrations that would not dampen and might go divergent. This kind of thing could tear the aircraft apart in flight.

Once we were confident the airplane was structurally stable dynamically, we started collecting structural fatigue data. Here we investigated how many strain applications the various structural members could manage before breaking. The best analogy for metal fatigue is the bending of a piece of hanger wire back and forth until it breaks. The number of cycles before failure at a specific load determined the fatigue strength.

Later, after I had left the company, during one of these low-altitude fatigue flights, test pilot Charlie Fisher had the entire vertical tail rip off the airplane. He managed to land using engine differential thrust for directional control. There's a famous picture of the B52 flying without its vertical stabilizer taken by a nearby F-100 Super Sabre fighter jet. It was the only time I had ever seen a vertical stabilizer come off a plane, that is until the crash of American Airlines Flight 587, which I would work on some thirty years later.

In addition to what I was learning on the B52 project, Wichita was an exciting aviation town. It was the home of several companies including Beech Aircraft, Cessna Aircraft, the old Stearman Aircraft Corporation, and the new Lear Jet Corporation. I did my best to get a look at each of them.

Learjet was the one that most piqued my interest. The Learjet was the second private jet airplane to be certified in the United States. For several years, the Learjet was synonymous with the term *private jet*. I later spent much time in the courtroom trying to redesign the airplane, but I had no idea how unstable and otherwise problematic the design was at the time.

While in Wichita, my strategy to get into the aircraft companies was to approach the front offices and suggest that I was writing an article for the school newspaper since I was also in engineering graduate school at Wichita State at the time. This often resulted in a tour of facilities, interviewing employees, and studying the company's airplanes. Too bad that it was before smartphones.

Most of the companies also had hangars on the airports or had their own landing strips. Since I had joined a local flying club, I had access to a number of small planes and used to fly throughout Kansas, landing in fields, on roads, and at the aircraft manufacturer's private strips. We did a lot of things with planes that are prohibited now. I was also developing some personal techniques for seeing the underbelly of airports and the plane manufacturers' plants, which would help me a great deal years later in the law practice. Rather than enter the airports through the terminal buildings, I'd go in with small planes and even bicycles.

One day, I took a flying club plane and landed on the Beech Aircraft landing strip at their plant in Wichita. When a line boy came out to ask, "Who are you with?" I made up a name, hoping he would say to himself, "Well, I don't know who he is, but I don't know everyone in the company, and if he is arriving by airplane, he must be somebody." It worked.

Many times, in the sixties and seventies, arriving by private plane gave a person an undeserved credibility. Sometimes when I showed up, I'd immediately be told to get back in my plane and go, but oftentimes, I wasn't thrown out until I had seen a great deal, talked to employees, and taken a lot of pictures with a mini camera.

As for getting to see the Learjet operation, I landed a flying club airplane at an FBO at Mid-Continent Airport where Lear was stationed and then took a fold-up bicycle from the back of the plane and rode it over to the Learjet facility from inside the airport property. One of the Learjet hangar doors was open. I leaned the bike up against the hangar wall, took a clipboard and pencil, and walked inside.

Immediately, a man with a white shirt, rolled-up sleeves, and tie came at me. I was scared. He said, "Son, I'm Mr. Lear. Stop standing around and get to work." My response was, "I don't work here. I am a graduate student at Wichita State University [which was true]. I'm writing an article for the school paper."

After hearing that, he seemed happy to get some press and started showing me around. During the tour, I learned a lot, including that the company had only two prototype airplanes that were being used for certification and that the Learjet was not yet in production. Some of what I learned that day paid off several years later in court. Before we finished the tour, he offered me a job, which is ironic since the Learjet Co. and I became regular adversaries.

Boeing 737

In December of 1962, my role in the B52 project was wound up at McConnell Air Force Base in Wichita, Kansas, and I was called back to Seattle, Boeing's headquarters. From time-to-time, we would fly down to Edwards Air Force Base in the Mojave Desert in Southern California to flight-test the C-135 military transport and KC-135, the refueling tanker version of the 135. Edwards was also known for its school, teaching aeronautics, and test pilots. I was lucky enough to audit several classes. I was very impressed by the teaching techniques. Several concepts were burned in my brain and are still fundamentals that I rely on today.

It was also refreshing, when doing design work on military planes, not to have marketing and economics meddling in the process. Yet there were some irritating political issues when dealing with military contracts as well.

Back up in Seattle, the work was so exciting. There were many jet airplanes being developed and tested. I regularly climbed up in the cockpits to study the instrument panels and read the operating manuals. Subsequently, I would often write memos to the various flight test groups with my thoughts and suggestions. Even though I dressed a bit Bohemian and had longer hair than the typical engineers, flight test management encouraged me and seemed happy with some of my ideas and performance.

About this time, I had the privilege to sit in on some of the initial meetings as a representative of flight test. Boeing was then in the preliminary design discussions of a short-haul or regional jet, which turned out to be the Boeing 737.

The first concept of the new airplane showed a two-engine jet with the engines attached beneath the wings. Looking at those sketches, I was immediately negative about the configuration. My first critical comment was that fan-jet engines are like giant vacuum cleaners and, positioned as they were, would pick up and ingest any trash on the airport.

But the biggest reason I had a negative opinion of the configuration was that the engines were too far out from the airplane centerline, which in the event of an engine failure would result in turning the airplane abruptly in the direction of the failed engine. The only way to control this asymmetry would be to have a large vertical tail-and-rudder system. But a large tail-and-rudder on this type of swept-wing airplane would aggravate Dutch roll and give too much roll authority to the rudder compared to the ailerons, which were intended to provide roll control. This tail design issue would come into play in a series of crashes in the 1990s, which I discuss at length in Chapter 14, "Tail Power." Suffice to say, in those days, I was making my opinions known.

In one of the meetings, I suggested bringing the engines in from the wings and placing them on the fuselage. Even though this was only a very preliminary design stage—the plane didn't even have a name—it seemed that the decision regarding the engines being out on the wings was fixed in concrete.

When I expressed my opinion, I was told that putting the engines inboard on the fuselage would make it look like a Douglas DC9, which was the competition—yes, Boeing still had competition then.

"Son," a senior member of the company said, I remember him dressed in an all-brown suit, "Boeing airplanes have their engines on the wings." It seemed obvious that allowing the placement of engines to be dictated by brand consideration and marketing was a bit foolish.

I was young and somewhat naive. I knew economics were important, but it was then that I came to understand that sound engineering could actually rank behind marketing and economics in airplane design. If I had gotten anything from the string of Detroit Jesuit schools I had attended as a teenager and young man, then it was a strong sense of ethical behavior. Sound economics and marketing or not, I could not see such a decision as ethical. I never could have predicted that the 737 would go on to become one of the most popular planes in history, which in many ways would bookend my lawyering and this story.

Although I was moving up the ladder in engineering flight test, it remained difficult to affect aircraft design. Probably this could be expected with me being a young employee in one of the world's major manufacturers, but as I looked outside of Boeing in my spare time, it seems clear that although the aircraft industry was obviously concerned with safety, many planes were lacking obvious and basic safety features. With airplanes starting to get bigger, like the Boeing 747, the result was going to be devastating crashes.

What would it be like to kill more than four hundred people at a time because of a marketing decision or cutting a corner?

My sense was that we needed to take safety more seriously. Just as I had felt the need to get out from behind the desk and climb the sky, I now felt like I could do more if I left Boeing.

The time was right for a move, and when Senator Barry Goldwater, a presidential hopeful for the 1964 election, bailed a Boeing 720 for use in his campaign, he shook my hand and uttered a few words that would send me on my way. He had announced he was running for president in January of that year and would secure his party's nomination at the convention in July.

The day he arrived I was suiting up for a flight test at the B52 hangar. He came around and shook everyone's hand and chatted for a moment. When he got to me, he asked, "Son, what are your career goals?"

Being flip, I replied, "I've always wanted to be a singer or a senator, but my friends tell me they would rather listen to me drink than sing."

The last thing he said was, "If you're really interested in politics, maybe you should go to law school," as he gave me the thumps-up and moved on.

I took his words to heart.

CHAPTER 2

Wolverine Air Charter

*I would uphold the law if for no other
reason but to protect myself.*

—Thomas More

Race Riots

In 1967, major race riots struck Detroit. It was the summer I graduated law school. They lasted five days in late July. Governor Romney called in the National Guard, and President Lyndon Johnson sent in the 101st Airborne Division. Thousands of people were arrested, handcuffed, and put on buses. Forty-three people were killed, while over a thousand were injured with something like two thousand buildings destroyed.

In the wake of the destruction, the city didn't have the resources to process all the people who had been arrested; Detroit specifically didn't have enough lawyers, and so the shortfall led the city to swear in my graduating class of lawyers and allow us to represent the people who had been arrested during the riots. I don't believe any of us had passed the bar exam at this point. I certainly had not. The early swearing-in also solved a problem: I knew I didn't want to work strictly in an office as a transactional lawyer, and the riots gave me the chance to bypass getting a "real" job and placed me in the center of the action. In courtrooms. I never looked back.

The National Guard was stationed on the steps of the Wayne County Criminal Courthouse, the Murphy Hall of Justice, with automatic rifles in hand in the summer heat. Reporters were hanging around looking for a scoop. In some neighborhoods, buildings were still smoldering, and defenders like myself had been assigned a busload of defendants each. The caseload was massive.

My clients' charges included rioting, assault, looting, breach of peace, destruction of property, theft, arson, and a litany of others. Every day and night for weeks, I was in that courthouse, getting the best deal I could find for my clients and also learning every step of the process. I found out that the city attorneys had a propensity to overcharge the African Americans, which helped me represent my clients later on down the line because I was learning how to play poker with these prosecutors. Learning when to walk away and when to take a plea. It was trial by fire but no better way to learn.

With that apprenticeship completed and all the connections I had made during the riots, which were many, the next step was to take the bar.

I had some political difficulties with the section of the exam on criminal and constitutional law as the questions were entirely related to Jimmy Hoffa and the Teamsters. These questions were asked from a pro-corporate perspective and that of the attorney general of the United States, Bobby Kennedy, looking for pro-government and pro-corporate answers.

I couldn't oblige. As I had moved from Seattle to the town of Lake Orion, a Teamsters town where Hoffa lived, and had gone to school with his son, my perspective on workers and unions had changed significantly.

I didn't answer the pertinent section of the bar in a manner acceptable at the time, and so I failed. I didn't like going along to get along, though I probably knew what they wanted to hear. I appealed the decision and lost. I thus had to take the test again and answered the way the bar wanted me to, but one thing was seared into my mind forever: corporate influence and its accompanying bias can be, are, and were systemic.

The lawyer side of my brain was churning. Most days, I commuted to work from Lake Orion to Detroit City Airport, right in the heart of "Motown," in a small airplane. I was learning that many basic safety items showing up on new automobiles, such as seat belts, padded dashboards, and other crashworthy devices, did not have their geniuses in the manufacturing companies but had been the result of car crashes and product liability lawsuits. I knew that we needed similar advances in airplane safety, but the cocktail of corporate malfeasance and bureaucratic complicity and inertia made that difficult. Someone needed to break the logjam. It would be mostly by and through lawsuits that this would happen.

I had left Boeing in the summer of '63 and immediately joined Continental Aviation and Engineering in Michigan, which later became Teledyne. The company headquarters was a stone's throw from City Airport. There I worked as a project engineer on a new line of turboshaft engines, which helped pay my way through night law school. But within a year of my return, I began a new business venture, which I was positive was going to succeed. Together with a pilot partner, I co-founded an air freight company named Wolverine

Air Charter. Though ill-fated, the undertaking would help me get my first airplane crash cases. This is where I really wanted to go.

Wolverine Air Charter

I had seen an opportunity when the Federal Aviation Administration began developing new regulations for the short-haul of passengers and freight in smaller aircraft-for-hire known as air taxi. Regional air service was seeing its share of growth, and the Midwest was dotted with small airfields and abandoned World War II military bases. Although the new short-haul regional airplanes needed improvement, I couldn't resist jumping in and becoming part of the exploding market.

In late 1964, I found a partner, a fellow pilot, and Wolverine Air Charter was formed. Together, we rented a one-room office in the brand-new Detroit City Airport Terminal building and acquired two airplanes. The first was a twin-engine Cessna model 310 with six seats; the second, a single-engine model 206 that also carried six. However, we usually took out the seats and carried freight. The airplanes were financed to the hilt. We had great hopes but very little capital.

I remember flying engineers in the Cessna 310 from Detroit to the National Aeronautics & Space Administration (NASA) in Virginia and also taking tourists up to Mackinaw Island, a state park in northern Michigan. Unfortunately, we weren't in operation all that long. My partner crashed while bringing a body to an undertaker in Detroit from upstate. He ran out of fuel and made an unscheduled landing in the woods at night and totally destroyed the airplane. Fortunately, he wasn't hurt.

Shortly after the crash, the bank repossessed the twin, and we were out of business. After that, I was left with the office in the terminal building at the airport, and while I didn't use it every day, when the riots were over it became my first law office. The door still had the sign reading Wolverine Air Charter. After I passed the state bar exam, some of my crazy pilot friends hung a sign under the Wolverine sign that read, "Honest Lawyer. *I win some of my cases.*" My first clients, however, still weren't aviation-related. For that I would need time and good fortune.

CHAPTER 3

Schifko

Mr. Gambini: All I ask from you is a simple answer to a very simple question.
There are only two ways to answer it: guilty or not guilty.

—*My Cousin Vinny*

The Jackson State Prison Band

Halbert Gene Turner was his name. He was doing life in Jackson State Prison in Michigan and was on trial again for murder. He was my client.

These were the days before "public defenders" offices. Persons charged with a crime who could not afford an attorney were assigned a lawyer by the court. Under the rules of ethics, the assigned lawyer was expected to take the case. The lawyer handling the indigent client was paid a set amount by the county. In my situation, being a young lawyer with three kids and without a connection to a law firm, I needed the money. So, I regularly hustled to have cases assigned to me.

The connections I had made during the Detroit riots helped, and my older brother was a very well-known young Catholic priest in a town that was politically Irish Catholic, which could help in some cases. I also spent a lot of time walking the back stairs and halls at the courthouse and asking the judges and clerks if they had any cases they needed to assign. The court housed as many as forty judges and their clerks, so there were plenty of people to talk to.

If I wasn't in the courtroom, then I was probably chasing a lead for a case. I took what I was given. The cases paid, but more importantly, I liked to be in court. The excitement and the human interactions and even the procedure and fear were my new passion. If I wasn't in trial, I would often sit in other courtrooms and watch attorneys' techniques, their theatrics, and the faces of the jurors. I now knew for certain that I could never have just pushed paper as a transactional lawyer or been stuck in some tower office in a corporation. I wanted to be around the courtroom and in the action, and I wanted it even if the cases weren't the types I had hoped for. On top of the experience, I was also able to help people who couldn't afford a lawyer.

Turner was one of these. But there was a problem. Halbert Gene Turner was a lifer. He had no desire to come to court or to help in his own defense. He was in for good anyway and was the band leader of the Jackson State Prison Band, the "Rooster Rooters," and the band was now his life. The time he spent defending himself was time away from band practice, which he didn't want to sacrifice, and whenever he came to court, he needed to be shackled because he was considered dangerous, which he also didn't like.

Turner had escaped from prison and had been shacked up with his old girlfriend and her two-year-old daughter in an apartment above a gas station. Before he was re-apprehended, he and the girlfriend had been accused of throwing the little girl down the stairs. The fall had killed the child. Both were charged with murder in the first degree, but the girlfriend had turned state's witness against her escapee boyfriend. It was a bad case, but it was what they had given me, and he was entitled to a defense. That was, to make the prosecution prove each element of the crime of first-degree murder beyond a reasonable doubt.

He may very well have been involved in causing the child to fall down the steps. But was it first-degree murder? Again, I was learning that it was normal to overcharge a defendant in criminal cases. This gave the state better leverage to get the defendant to plead guilty to a lesser charge and save time and the cost of a trial by jury. In this case, the proper charge would have been something like manslaughter since first-degree murder needed to fulfill three elements: (1) the unjustifiable taking of the life of another, (2) premeditation, and (3) malice of forethought.

It was my job to make the prosecution prove "beyond a reasonable doubt" that each of the elements of murder in the first degree had been met.

As a preliminary step, I decided I should talk with the girlfriend. I had a few questions I wanted resolved. As it turned out, she lived in a bad neighborhood in Monroe, Michigan. After tracking her down and asking around, I found her with some kids at Detroit Beach on Lake Erie. I introduced myself and told her I wanted to talk. She seemed startled.

"I can't talk here," she said. "Let's go to my apartment."

I agreed.

She lived nearby on the top floor of an old four-family flat. The only access was up the fire escape and through a window, which was how I entered. We talked a few minutes. I mostly asked questions, and she answered, and at one point, she either grew tired of my questioning or took issue with what I had asked because she started screaming, "Rape! Rape!" at the top of her lungs.

I dove out the window and ran down the steel fire escape, hitting every third or fourth step on the way. I didn't want to explain to a police officer what had happened, or a neighbor. No one else seemed to notice though, and I quickly got into my car, briefcase in hand, and sped from the apartment's parking lot. This was a piece of reconnaissance that had gone badly for me.

Personally, talking with witnesses had become a habit; it was part of my method, like investigating aeronautical businesses from the runway side of the hangar. You might just call it curiosity. In this case, it nearly killed the cat. But my client's girlfriend gave me a new respect for how careful I needed to be in conducting my own investigations and how much trouble I might get in if I wasn't. I might hire a private detective in the future, but where would the fun in that be? This particular meeting didn't hurt my case any more than it was already troubled from the outset by Turner and his own actions or lack thereof.

He was found guilty in the first trial, but I had the conviction reversed since the prosecution had shown pictures of the two-year-old girl dead on a slab in the morgue. The Supreme Court of the State of Michigan had spoken to this issue. You can't inflame a jury with gross pictures in that way. At the second trial, we got a hung jury. The third time around, Turner pleaded guilty to manslaughter, likely the proper charge in the first place. He didn't want to spend any more time away from the Jackson Rooster Rooters, and he was already serving life in prison, so defending himself had become too big of a hassle.

"You did what you could, Dick," he told me.

I seemed to care more than he did. Who likes to lose? But I had come away learning a lesson or two concerning the courts, criminals, and regarding human nature, as well as when and when not to be alone with a woman.

Soon after, I was assigned a second murder case. It would give me more than experience. Again, the plea-bargaining system was misused by prosecutors. In this way, there were two tiers of justice: one for those who could afford good representation and one for everybody else. The result was the defendant would plead guilty to a lesser charge out of fear of taking a chance in court where, if he lost, he would be most likely facing a loss of his liberty.

In the case of the *State of Michigan v. James Daski*, my client was charged with first-degree murder for a bar fight, which I thought was absurd. They should never have charged him with first-degree. But the courts simply didn't have the staff to try every case, and this was one way of winnowing down the caseload.

In the Daski trial, two things happened. The first was that Daski didn't think I was old enough to represent him. He wanted a more experienced lawyer but the court was not going to give him one. He threatened me then, which was disconcerting since he had recently killed a man by stabbing him with the jagged end of a broken pool cue. No matter what I did in his favor, he didn't like me and didn't trust me. Fortunately, I was able to persuade the jury not to give a bar fight the dignity of a murder trial.

He was acquitted. But Daski continued to be moody and uncooperative throughout the remainder of the procedure. He was so belligerent the judge held him in contempt for not cooperating with counsel. The judge then congratulated me for how I handled the case. That was the second thing that happened in this trial: I made friends with the judge and got to know his law clerk.

His name was Judge Montante. We ended up developing a lifetime relationship. He would later call me when he was writing opinions and ask for mine on certain points of law. He also had a fantastic law clerk by the name of Vicky Heldman, who was preparing for the bar exam then. Little did I know she would be my future law partner. But I needed some cases of my own before I could even dream of having a partner.

When I was young teenager, I got hooked on skiing, although it was hardly a sport that I could afford. One weekend, I had hitchhiked up to Boyne Mountain Ski Area in northern Michigan. This trip really was a turn of fate. I was using a pair of Army surplus skis and an old army jacket, equally out of fashion. It was what I could afford. But I had the good luck to sit beside an older lawyer on the chairlift. Boyne is not a big mountain. It has a vertical rise of some five hundred feet, so our ride up was not long, but we had enough time to have a conversation.

The man beside me introduced himself as Al Lopatin of Lopatin & Miller. I knew the name. Most of the lawyers in Detroit would have known it too. He was a well-known plaintiff's attorney in Michigan, probably the most well-known.

We started talking, and I told him I had four kids, that I was just out of law school, and that I was having trouble making a living. I also mentioned what I had been doing down at the courts and the cases I had worked and how I had gotten them, so he had some idea of my experience, or maybe just sensed my passion and enthusiasm.

He told me to come down to his office, that he had a number of cases that I could have if I wanted. He explained that he would front the cost, and we'd split the contingency fee if we were successful. It sounded like a good deal; I was excited. It certainly was a good break, and while it wouldn't guarantee an income, it gave me cases and put me in the courtroom. These were odds I liked.

Al Lopatin

Al would become a mentor. I also didn't know that he was famous for taking cases from people who came in off the street and that he rarely turned anyone away when he felt they had been wronged.

This habit meant that he helped people who needed it; it also meant he took on a lot of really bad cases, some so bad they were humorous. The clients were also underdogs, which I appreciated. But some of the bad ones were really, very bad. In one instance, the plaintiff had been hit by a car—at least he claimed he had been. He further claimed that his father was in a mental institution, his mother was dying, and he was working two jobs, one at Ford and one at a steel factory to support his family. Only part of that was true, or at least it was never proven untrue.

I put him on the stand, and he told his story before the jury. I watched their reactions. I thought he was convincing, and his story had a good effect on jurors.

Later that night, the defense attorney phoned me. There was a sense of camaraderie between lawyers at that time that I think has largely gone away. When I answered the phone, the attorney said, "Your client's lying through his teeth. He never worked at the steel company and he was fired from Ford for using drugs. I'm going to catch him on the stand tomorrow."

I thanked him for passing that information on before springing it on me in court. I hung up and called Al. He was gambling in Monte Carlo. It took some time, but I got through to him at the hotel. I picture him dressed in a tuxedo, phone in hand, standing by the ornate cage in the casino lobby.

"Al," I said when I finally got through, "the case is a piece of junk. He's lying." I went on to explain why.

"Just try it," he said. "Quit whining." Then he hung up and returned to the roulette table or whatever he had been doing.

I didn't have much time to come up with something, so I called the client and asked why he had been lying. He didn't answer at first, then he started to double-talk me. I stopped him and said, "I'm going to put you on the stand tomorrow. Tell the truth." He didn't know how to respond.

Tomorrow came, and I did exactly as I said, "Did you tell the truth on the stand yesterday"? I asked him after he had been sworn in.

He said, "No."

I asked him why he had lied to the jury. He seemed remorseful and sullen and then began to tell his story. He said he needed the money, that he was supporting his family, but he didn't have a job, and the accident made it impossible for him to get one now.

I watched the jury closely as he spoke. A man who admits he has been lying usually loses all credibility. But he was endearing and I could see the jury was at least listening. Getting through to the jurors was everything in a trial like this one.

Afterward, they deliberated for a short time and returned. It was a hung jury, probably the best outcome we could have hoped for under the circumstances. Had the lawyer for the defense not called and told me my client was lying, the decision would have been unanimous against us. Putting the client on the stand and getting him to admit he was lying at least helped salvage what could be salvaged, and we did it without misrepresenting the case.

I felt that I was starting to get a feel for juries then, at least those in Wayne County. These people were generally from the inner city and fairly poor. They often saw the courts and insurance companies as the establishment and were anxious to play Robin Hood and take from the rich and give to the poor. But I would later learn the hard way that a jury in Wayne County is much different from those in federal courts and other venues throughout the country.

I also learned just how careful I had to be with Al's clients. Many were solid, but several were beyond lost. Still, I took what he would give me because I might win. I needed the experience, and I didn't yet have enough cases of my own, so I would field what he gave me, and sometimes the weird ones worked out.

"Did Richard leave for the day?" I remember him shouting over the loudspeaker in his four-story office building.

"Yes!" I shouted back. Everyone in the building could hear the conversation.

"You want to do a douche powder case?" he asked.

Some of the other attorneys in the building might have thought he was losing his grip. As it turned out, the powder contained alum and had burned a woman, our client, when she was in the shower. It was a real case. The powder was dangerous; there was no question about it. The subject also lent levity to the courtroom, which helped me connect to the jury.

I remember telling them she had left the shower like "Apollo left the launchpad." They laughed. We won. If you could make a jury laugh, it was usually positive, and I was learning those subtleties the only way you can by getting a feel for juries themselves and from other lawyers. It would pay dividends later when I started to handle airplane crash cases, which was still a bit of a dream even though I had the office at the airport.

We could also be more theatrical in trial then. A later partner of mine, Richard Goodman, son of Ernie Goodman, used to go to the back of the courtroom and lean his head on the wall, sometimes banging it against the paneling, distracting from the other side as they were making the case. And one attorney, Paul Valentino, whom I would later fly to South America with in a replica of Amelia Earhart's plane, fired a gun in the court. When I brought a case against GM claiming, among other things, that the Corvette was a flammable car, I lit a piece of a fiberglass fender on fire for the jury. There was a lot of smoke and flames, and the judge started banging his gavel. These days, you might be disbarred, but at the time, antics like these were part of a trial lawyer's toolbox. I learned a lot of these tricks on the job or spontaneously based on stories that I had read about famous trial lawyers like Clarence Darrow, Melvin Belli, and others. Maybe most important: don't ever be cocky and be humble.

I spent every day, all day, at court trying cases good and bad. Like a revolving door, I would finish closing arguments in one trial and walk down the hall and give an opening statement in another. It was small time stuff, most had nothing to do with airplanes or engineering, but I was getting more trial experience than practically anyone in the country. I was winning, even with the odds against me. It was neither legal nor ethical to advertise in those days. Thus, media coverage was of great value.

Bigger cases were coming. Soon I'd get a six-figure verdict for a wrongful death case. A woman's husband had died of asphyxiation while working inside a sewer for the city of Monroe, Michigan, not far south of Detroit on the western end of Lake Erie, near where I had made the rapid exit from the top floor apartment in the Turner murder case.

The verdict awarded the plaintiff eight hundred thousand dollars. She more than deserved the money too. Her husband's death could have been prevented if the city had used reasonable care under the circumstances. This one made the newspapers, and recognition like that was important since, as I said, lawyers weren't permitted to advertise in those days, which would only come later.

The verdict marked a big win for us. Lopatin was happy. So was I. He would have made me partner, in fact, but as it turned out, it was a Jewish law firm. All his partners were Jewish. They had been under the impression I was Jewish too. When they learned I wasn't, they weren't going to vote me in as a partner. They had a deal between themselves to that effect. But that didn't end our relationship.

It reminds me, before the partnership issue came up, I was in trial with one of Al's partners, and during jury selection, I was angling to have one of the women on the panel removed, but Al's partner leaned over to me and said, "We want to keep her. She's Jewish, and sooner or later, she's going to find out you and I are Jewish too." I didn't bother telling him otherwise.

Not being partner was better for me in the end. It fit my needs and let me acquire my own cases and build my own firm using not just my court experience but my engineering education. Yet, it still wasn't clear how I would go from A to Z and work airplane cases. All I could do was to keep trying cases and make connections.

With the verdicts I was getting and the fact I nearly lived at court, making connections wasn't hard. I still entered through the rear of the building and used the back stairs and halls, where I could run into the clerks and secretaries.

Some memorable days I would join the older and more successful lawyers either at the London Chop House or the Caucus Club. There were three courthouses downtown: the Murphy Hall of Justice for most criminal cases, the Wayne County Circuit Court, and the Traffic Court. All were in walking distance to the Chop House and the Caucus Club, which were filled with lawyers and judges. It was like a fraternal organization or a beehive, which helped build the sense of camaraderie.

There was a lot to learn at these places, both old court stories and fresh news, plenty of jokes, story swapping, and bragging. The type of thing you don't get at school, or at a firm, but is good to have filed away. There were various scams running at any given time too, and it was wise to know it beforehand if they crossed your desk. There were the regular stories and criticism of the ambulance chasers. One scam had city cops selling fake police reports to seedy lawyers to participate in insurance fraud; there were others as well. These were the kinds of things you might learn.

It was then, either in the back halls of the court or at one of the local restaurants, that I met Ernie Goodman. Ernie was a well-known civil rights attorney then. I became friendly with him, and he was something of a mentor. His son would later become a partner of mine. Ernie told a joke about how he had invented product liability law to fund his social causes like defending the Black Panthers and the prisoners in the Attica Prison Riots. Product liability had been long in coming to the United States, and while Ernie hadn't really invented it, discussing its brief history in American courts helped move me to the next stage.

Product Liability

From the law side of my brain, I could see that product liability, a new and developing area of tort law, was gaining momentum in the courts. The old defense, formerly used by manufacturers, known as "caveat emptor," or "let buyer beware," was losing ground. Manufacturers and sellers of dangerous and defective products were beginning to be more regularly sued for the devastating effect of their wares.

Likewise, the relatively new Uniform Commercial Code (UCC) included language that was being used to support this growing area of tort law. Within the UCC, you could find language that stated that a product was impliedly warrantied to be fit for its intended purpose. The language in the UCC was statutory law. Much of published precedent arising out of product liability cases initially cited this code in support of implied warranty of "fitness for intended purpose." As a result, we began to see products improving and become safer through lawsuits.

I felt more and more that I could design and/or redesign airplanes in the courtroom.

At this time, Ralph Nader had become a major pain to General Motors. He published his book *Unsafe at Any Speed*, dealing with GM's Corvair, a seminal moment that came right as product liability verdicts were beginning to change the design of automobiles. Crash testing, seat belts, shoulder harnesses, padded dashboards, collapsible steering wheels, and airbags all had their genesis in the courtroom, not from the companies themselves or regulators who worked closely together. In the courts, large verdicts were making products safe. The auto industry was grudgingly making design changes, and the government was starting to enact regulatory administrative laws requiring automobiles to meet new safety standards including "crashworthy" standards.

It was becoming clear that courts and jury verdicts could affect engineering design. Law could save lives. Lawsuits, through verdicts, were affecting design standards and the regulatory law that set the standards for so many consumer products, such as automobiles, appliances, toys, and, yes, airplanes. The United States Code of Federal Regulations (CFRs) Part 14, Sections 23 and 25 set the design standards for airplanes. I saw these as the minimum standards. I believed that the design standards needed to be much higher in the area of safety. The interface between the flying machines and people had to be less risky. The design of these products had to better serve the needs of humankind.

Up to this time, the growing area of product liability law involved primarily manufacturing defects such as a loose bolt, a piece of bad metal, or a broken part. My thoughts naturally focused more on the design stage of the product. What was the design criteria? What kind of issues should have been included in the initial phase of the design process? That is, what kind of issues should prudent engineers consider and include as part of the design criteria? So often, the problem was in the initial design process as compared to the manufacturing process. The design process had to consider possible failure modes and provide redundancy. Accidents and crashes had to be considered from the outset of the design process and have a focus on protection of the occupants.

I then knew I could have traction and put my first career to use. I could see where the law was going and why it had to go there. We're talking flawed designs that would foreseeably cause death and injury.

One of my early product liability cases dealt with such a design issue.

I tried a case against Caterpillar involving one of their machines: a hauling scraper. These very large Earth-moving machines were used to reshape the terrain. Construction workers with shovels and hand tools would be working on the ground in the immediate vicinity of these machines. In this case, the Caterpillar operator had run over one of the workers. The man had lost his leg. The trouble was that the machine had such poorly designed sight lines that it left a massive and needless blind spot. The driver simply couldn't see the people whom everybody knew would be working around the hauling scraper. The accident was foreseeable. The machine also gave no warning when it started to move.

This case was tried in a temporary courthouse down the street from the usual Wayne County location as construction was ongoing. The hauling scraper case was one of two cases I tried there.

A friend of mine, Bill Bower, who co-owned an airplane with me, had also just graduated engineering school. I told him I wanted him to testify as an expert witness and explained the case. He testified to what the design criteria should have been for a machine like that, operating with men around it on the ground. The testimony went well.

To further make a point, I had a large piece of cardboard cutout in the shape of the blind spot, which we marked "blind spot," and used it as an exhibit. Every night, the bailiff would put the blind spot away. Every morning when trial began, I'd say to the judge, "Your Honor, can we bring out the blind spot?" He would then call for it, and the large cardboard cutout marked "blind spot" would be marched back out in front of the jury.

It proved effective. The jury liked it. We got a great result for the plaintiff. Another of this case's outcomes, and other cases like it, was that large machinery, like the hauling scraper, were required to have an audible warning when they began to move and were underway.

Norbert Schifko

At about the same time, in fact, Norbert Schifko was the other case tried in the provisional courtroom that Al Lopatin handed me which would be my biggest win to date. But this case was no laughing matter. It was a rear-impact fire case in a Ford LTD station wagon where a man's son had died.

The incident happened in October of 1972. The driver, Norbert Schifko, his wife, and their son and daughter were pulling out of a restaurant parking lot in Livonia, Michigan, when their car was rear-ended by a car driven by Martin Andrew Pedlar, who was seventeen at the time. The gas tank on Schifko's station wagon ruptured and the cabin was engulfed in flames within seconds. Mr. Schifko's twelve-year-old son, Bobby, was pinned in the back seat. His leg was trapped. Schifko tried to pull him out but couldn't. Bobby died shouting, "I'm stuck. Dad, help me."

He watched his twelve-year-old son burn to death. Schifko would never be the same. He himself suffered severe burns on his face and legs, requiring surgery. He couldn't walk for months afterward and had a heart attack two years later.

The trial took seven weeks. This was not Ford Motor Company's first experience with a devastating post-impact fire in one of its cars. The company had an extensive history with this type of devastating accident. To Ford, this was a "foreseeable event." It should have been dealt with at the design stage and evaluated by conducting crash tests before putting these vehicles on the market. In response to this and other such verdicts, the industry has substantially redesigned fuel storage systems.

This case had an interesting side story. I was cross-examining a senior engineer who had become part of management at Ford. I asked him to explain to the jury what was required to start a fire. His response was fuel, air, and ignition.

I followed up. "That is not exactly accurate, is it? It actually requires oxygen, doesn't it?"

He responded, "Well, air is mostly oxygen."

The fact is that air is only about 21 percent oxygen and 77 some percent nitrogen and some other inert gases. His error was picked up by the nightly news.

The Schifko case was a record jury verdict in Michigan for the wrongful death of a single minor, which further helped advance safety in automobiles. While it couldn't bring Mr. Schifko's son back, it at least helped bring a modicum of closure. And importantly thereafter, more crash testing was required by federal regulatory laws.

But something else happened in the time it had taken me to bring Schifko to trial in late 1976.

I had picked up some airplane crash cases. Initially, these were general aviation crashes. The term *general aviation* pertains to small planes used by corporations and private citizens as compared to airlines. In those days, it generally referred to planes under 12,500 pounds maximum allowable takeoff weight and less. Today it applies to much larger aircraft, including rather large private and corporate jets.

CHAPTER 4

Cessna's Flat Spin

And done a hundred things
You have not dreamed of --- wheeled
and soared and swung
High in the sunlit silence.

—*"High Flight" by John Gillespie Magee*

The Lutes Case

It was May 13, 1972. Far above Highway 24 near the small town of Metamora, Michigan, a single-engine Cessna 150 Aerobat was spinning toward the ground. To the casual observer driving north on the highway, it might have appeared that the pilot was having a lot of fun. But the airplane never recovered from the spin and crashed into a cornfield not far from the road, killing the two young men inside. Much of the flight, including the spin and the crash, had been captured by the passenger, Robert Lutes, on an eight-millimeter movie camera from the cockpit.

The question was: Why hadn't the pilot been able to recover? I had some ideas!

A while back, I had gotten into a spin in a small airplane on my own. I had an instant unintended vision of my own fate and started pushing and pulling everything in the cockpit. By some quirk unknown to me, the plane recovered and started behaving itself and flying like an airplane should. I decided then that if I was going to play in bird land, I needed to fully understand the mechanics of spinning and spin recovery. If nothing else, I learned that both airplane design and the pilot played a part in the recovery.

My office was still at Detroit City Airport. I had been receiving some pretty good press lately arising out of trying assigned criminal cases, the Al Lopatin cases, and a few other civil cases. I suspect this noise was what motivated Carol Lutes, the surviving widow of Robert and the mother of two, now-fatherless children, to come to my office shortly after the fatal crash of the Cessna 150 Aerobat.

I was dismayed when I watched the eight-millimeter footage taken from the cockpit. From my experience, the literature I had read, and what I saw on the film, I believed this was more than a simple case of pilot error. The Lutes case wasn't the first case I tried where I studied the aerodynamic spin issue. Just prior, I had tried a jury case involving a Cessna model 170. That model was slightly bigger and carried four instead of two people. Additionally, it was a tail dragger instead of a tricycle landing gear configuration. Although the C-170 didn't have the spin recovery problem suffered by the C-150 and C-150 Aerobat, it did have a tendency to enter an incipient spin when a pilot was trying to recover from a stall, intentionally or otherwise. This case was another experience which had brought me to study the characteristics of spins.

The plaintiff in the C-170 case was at a low altitude and stalled unintentionally on departure and hit the ground while in an incipient spin. I had already looked at the FAA and NTSB data available with regard to stall/spin accidents. It turned out that in 1972, the NTSB had released a special study of stall/spin accidents in small general aviation aircraft where they mentioned that the Cessna 150 had a "very high" stall/spin accident rate. That information hadn't helped me in the 170 case, but I recalled it now, and I wanted to find out why.

Recovery Problem

Hanging around at airports with pilots, mechanics, and other airport bums, I found out that Cessna had changed the vertical tail in the early sixties. After that, it seemed the spin recovery problem got substantially worse. This information certainly didn't prove what had happened, but it was a pretty good starting point. The next step was to do some detailed research, tests, and analysis on my own to find out why spin recovery was such a problem in the 150.

To start, aerodynamic spins are a natural phenomenon of single-engine airplanes. They occur when the angle of attack (that is, the angle between the wing and the relative wind) gets too high and the air flowing over the upper surface can no longer stay attached to the upper surface of the wing. The result is that the wing quits flying or is said to stall. If one wing loses its lift before the other or some control surface starts a turn, one wing can drop, and the plane begins to spin. It looks somewhat like a spiral, but the wing is not flying, that is, it is not producing any lift.

By the time I took on the Lutes case, I had flown most all of Cessna's aircraft. Some were flying club airplanes, others were clients, and I had been a partner in the ownership of a few of the older models. All told, I had flown the 120, 140, 145, 150, 170, 172, 182, 205, and the 210. Initially, the single-engine airplanes were built with a straight vertical tail. But at some point, the Piper Aircraft Company put a swept-back vertical tail on their Cherokee. This was apparently to make it look faster and sexier. Cessna followed suit and put a jaunty-sweep on the vertical tail of its C-150.

I knew the sweep was likely the problem, and I had a hunch that they had neither analyzed its effect on the stability and control of the airplane nor properly tested it. Additionally, there was talk around the airports that the C-150 with the swept-back tail had two spin modes. It was said that one was quite steep and the other quite flat. The normal recovery procedure for a spin is full opposite rudder and a brisk forward movement on the stick or yoke.

Unfortunately, this didn't work well when trying to recover from a flat spin in the Cessna 150 with the swept-tail. A flat spin in this plane was often be followed by a strong odor in the cockpit and terror on the face of the pilot.

I began my case preparation by building a small wooden, but to scale, model of the C-150 with the swept-tail modification. First, I played with the model in front of the kitchen fan. From these simple tests, I came to believe that the problem was due to the swept-tail's shape in that the rudder was blocked out by the horizontal stabilizer (little rear wing) during a flat spin.

Since I had some access to the wind tunnel at the aero-engineering department at the University of Detroit, my next step was to do some more sophisticated model testing. These tests revealed that the rudder was mostly blocked out by the horizontal stabilizer in a flat spin, which made the rudder ineffectual.

It wasn't as if the spin characteristics of small airplanes were unknown. In our research, we found that there had been extensive studies on airplane spin properties conducted by the National Advisory Commission for Aeronautics (NACA), the precursor of NASA. These tests were conducted in the late 1930s and early 1940s. The final report titled "Tail Design Requirements for Satisfactory Spin Recovery," issued in 1946, analyzed spin data on one hundred model military airplanes tested in the free-spinning wind tunnels at Langley, Virginia.

Recovery in two full turns or less, while the plane is in a normal spin maneuver, was considered satisfactory. This NACA report was a treasure of information for an airplane design team. In the fifties and sixties, NACA Technical Notes and Reports were among the main reference tools industry-wide for airplane design. The 1946 report used the term *TDPF* (*tail damping power factor*). It was determined that the ability to recover from a spin is related to the weight and geometry of the airframe and the power of certain flight controls. It seemed obvious to me that the design of the Cessna 150 Aerobat, which had the swept-back tail, failed to have an acceptable TDPF. But I needed more than this thirty-year-old report if I was going to prove it.

What I needed was a video of a real live attempt to recover from a flat spin in a swept-tail C-150.

Spin Test

Don Sommer was a friend of mine whom I knew from the airfields around Detroit. He was an engineer, a great pilot, and a FAA-rated airplane mechanic. I would say Don was a "real good stick" as in "stick and rudder." He also knew how to evaluate an airplane's maneuvers and had testified as an expert witness in the previous Cessna 170 case involving the incipient spin where he did some exceptional flight testing for that case. Although he looked young, he knew his stuff.

He had a good understanding of the various Cessna models too since he was also a Cessna dealer. I was confident that he could do the job. We met and planned to put the spin issue on film. We borrowed our test airplane from one of Don's customers.

I understood that Don had told the owner that we were going to perform several spins and make a film. However, the customer may have had second thoughts about letting us use his plane had he seen Don climb aboard wearing a parachute.

The day we chose for the spin flight turned out to be a fine one with a clear sky and low wind. Don took off on a 2,200-foot strip at the Lake Orion Airport about six in the morning. The plan was for me to lay on the ground in a field near the airport with an eight-millimeter movie camera. He would climb to 6,000 feet and enter a spin. We would be in radio contact. After six turns, I would call out a recovery technique.

So was the plan.

I took my place on the ground with the camera, and he climbed to altitude. At the agreed altitude, he increased the angle of attack, stalled, and entered a spin. As we had planned, it was nice and flat. I began to count the turns out loud. "One, two, three . . ." By the fourth turn, I was becoming concerned. Now with each turn, the rotations grew tighter and faster. At turn six, I called for a full opposite rudder and a brisk forward movement on the stick. This was our agreed recovery procedure. The turns continued. They grew tighter and faster. As I counted seven, eight, I thought, *My god! I've killed this man.*

All of a sudden, I saw something strange. It looked like the airplane might be coming apart. Then the nose went down and the plane entered a normal spin recovery, very close to the ground. He landed on the nearby runway.

When he climbed out of the aircraft, he said with a cool head, "I learned something," and then added, "Did you get it all on film?"

I responded with a shaky voice, "It looked like the airplane was coming apart."

"Oh, that was probably when I opened the door," he responded.

"The door?"

"I took my seat belt off and jumped forward to move center of gravity forward. What you saw was me opening the door."

"Why?" I blurted out. "Were you going to jump?"

"No," he exclaimed. He said that when he was training in a seaplane, they taught us how to sail on the water using the door as a sail. He decided to use it as a flight control to slow down the spin. I am not sure the door acting as a sail was the answer, but coupled with jumping onto the instrument panel the plane recovered. Moving the center of gravity forward brought the nose down and effectively changed the spin to the steep mode, from which recovery was much more likely.

I was happy he was alive. He certainly tried everything to recover that plane. The video would make a great piece of demonstrative evidence.

The World Aerobatic Champion

We tried the case in Detroit in the Wayne County Circuit Court before the Honorable James Montante.

Vicki Heldman, who had been a law clerk for Judge Montante during the Daski murder case, was now my law partner and a very valuable asset in preparing for a trial. Vicki was a great legal writer of pleadings and briefs, and she also presented the proofs of loss to the Lutes family of their father and breadwinner.

The defendants were the Cessna Aircraft Company of Wichita, Kansas, and Commander Flight Service of Pontiac, Michigan. The attorney for the defendant Cessna was none other than Bill Cooney, whom I had faced previously in the Beechcraft case. He had settled with me then, which I thought might have been out of friendship to my father as they were both church ushers together.

Bill Cooney was a good and successful trial defense lawyer. He was tall, well-spoken, handsome, and always well-dressed in a dark suit, looking very corporate. The insurance companies loved him. I am sure that he was one of the major rainmakers, bringing lots of business into the silk-stocking firm of Plunkett, Cooney, Rutt, and Peacock.

Like *My Cousin Vinny*, I was still wearing that seventeen-dollar, three-piece corduroy suit from Sears, Roebuck & Company. In my alleged mind, the contrast between Mr. Cooney's classic and polished persona and my own appearance might work to my advantage with the inner-city working-class jurors. By this time, Vicki and I had become very close to Judge Montante, within the bounds of propriety. We knew him to be tough but fair. Montante was a short, distinctly Italian man standing about five feet two inches tall.

He had some interesting character traits. When he got a little upset or angry, he would climb and stand on the seat of his chair behind the bench. He had two gavels. One quite large and another tiny. He used to pick up the large one and tell the jury, "This one is for big cases and serious matters, and this little one is for lesser matters." When he really wanted to get a case settled, he would invite the lawyers for both sides into his chambers where he had a little putting green.

Both lawyers were requested to write their drop-dead number on a little yellow sticky note and put them upside down on his desk. There then would be a putting contest to see who won. The case was settled accordingly.

I was hoping to win a verdict in the Lutes case rather than settle it, and it appeared that Cessna didn't want to settle either. A product liability case claiming defective design as compared to a defect in the manufacturing process was a relatively new concept at this point in time. While it was something they weren't used to, I saw design cases as compared to a claim of a broken part, bad metal or loose screw, as being more difficult to defend. It was hard for the defendant to get their arms around it since design has to do with concepts and the product of the engineering mind. That is, what was the right way to serve the needs and the safety of the user. It was also an aspect that the corporate culture was so often overlooking.

Dr. Jack Fairchild, PhD, an aeronautical engineering professor at the University of Texas, was the first expert witness I called. I had met Jack not long before on a warm night playing night tennis under the lights in Fort Worth, Texas. After challenging him to a set of singles, which he won, we sat and talked about airplanes. He told me how he and his students had designed and were building a small experimental airplane of a unique configuration that he referred to as a Canard.

I told him about the Lutes case and my claim about the swept-tail diminishing the spin recovery capabilities. Based on that discussion, I thought he might be a great choice to explain aerodynamic spinning and recovery to a jury. After one more set of tennis, he agreed to testify and give his opinion with regard to the design.

Dr. Fairchild was great, and the jury clearly saw him as a teacher. I was quite sure that these six women sitting in the box now understood the basics of an aerodynamic spin of a small single-engine airplane. Dr. Fairchild also opined that the design of the Cessna Aerobat was defective. It was very difficult for Mr. Cooney to cross or discredit Fairchild. Further still, it seemed the jury was unhappy that he appeared to be a bit disrespectful to this kind and humble professor.

My next expert was Mr. Bowman. He had been an engineer for NACA in the 1930s and was active in the Langley spin tunnel. At the time, he was quite elderly. However, he was sharp and clear in explaining tail-damping power factor to the jury. He told them this term was the best algorithm for designing for spin recovery.

Don Sommer was next. He laid the foundation for introducing our spin and recovery demo movie and further drew a comparison with Robert Lutes's eight-millimeter film.

When I had used Sommer in the Cessna 170 case a year before, he looked so young and baby-faced that I was concerned that he lacked the image of a wise and sage expert. For this case, I had him grow a beard and dress a bit more professorial. Now he seemed to play the part well.

When it was time for cross-examination, Cooney was ready to tear into him.

He started, "Isn't it true, Mr. Sommer, that the Cessna model 150 airplane was certified as being airworthy by the Federal Aviation Administration of the United States government?"

Sommer responded, "Well, that's not exactly true, Mr. Cooney."

Next, Cooney said very loudly, "How can you say that? You must admit that it was the FAA themselves that deemed this very airplane as airworthy."

Sommer said, "Let me show you, the court, and the jury the actual airworthiness certificate from the airplane that killed Robert Lutes. You will notice that it is signed-off by a man named Obed Wells. Mr. Wells also happens to be an employee of the Cessna Aircraft Company." Don had done his homework. By mentioning this now, it appeared to the jury that the Cessna Airplane Company itself had signed its own airworthiness certificate.

At this point, we had made a "prima facie" case, a legal term meaning that there was sufficient evidence to let the jury decide for the plaintiff if they chose. Our proofs highlighted a defective design in that the defendant designed and built an aerobatic plane expressly represented as capable of performing and safely recovering from spins using normal recovery procedures, but that it was not actually capable of recovering using normal procedures. At this stage of the trial, there was prima facie evidence of a design defect and that it had caused the death of Robert Lutes. We were headed in the right direction, and I had a good vibe from the jury.

Now it was the defense's turn to call a witness. Judge Montante, addressing the defense, stood up on his chair. "Call your first witness," he said.

Cooney played safe at first and used Cessna employees to testify to their own merits and made a big point of showing how the 150 Aerobat was affectively certified by the Federal Aviation Administration and met all the design and manufacturing standards.

But he had already tried to take this path with Don Sommer. I would make more use of it in cross-examination. The fact that their certification had actually been signed by one of their own employees was an ugly fact. It didn't make it any better that the FAA designated a Cessna company employee to act on its behalf, known as a DMIR (designated manufacturing inspection representative). It just sounded like a bureaucratic way of explaining why the fox was allowed inside the henhouse, a pattern I was beginning to recognize.

Cooney had an ace up his sleeve, which he must have hoped would turn the case in their favor since he had kept it secret until now.

"The defense calls Mr. Charles Hillard to the stand," Cooney said. "Will you step forward and be sworn in?"

This Hillard was a damn handsome man, wearing a tan suede sport coat and hair like Fonzie. He leaned forward toward the all-female jury. I wondered if this would have an effect.

Cooney said, "Will you introduce yourself to the jury?"

"Yes, sir. My name is Charles Hillard. However, most call me Charlie H."

"What is your profession, Charlie H?"

Trying to act humble, he lowered his head somewhat and said, "I am a professional aerobatic pilot."

"Please, Mr. Charlie H, don't be so modest. You are in fact the world's aerobatic champion, aren't you?"

He responded with a, "Well, yes."

Vicki handed me a quick note suggesting that I object to him testifying. He had neither been listed in the pretrial statement nor had he filed an expert witness report as required by the court rules.

Now I had never heard of Charlie Hillard and was quite chagrined that I didn't know who the world's aerobatic champ was. I also had no idea what he might say other than to explain how the Cessna 150 Aerobat was the best of the best. Vicki was correct in that, if we were playing by the book, I should certainly object, but I had a gut feeling that his testimony might be good for us and let him begin without objection.

As I had suspected, Charlie sang the praises of the Aerobat. That was fine. He was obviously very knowledgeable about aeronautical maneuvers and the use of flight controls, and I began to think that maybe I could turn him and make him effectively my expert.

So, when Cooney yielded the witness to me for cross-examination, I opened with, "Mr. Hillard, the court, the jury, and I want to thank you so much for taking time from your very busy schedule to come and share your extensive knowledge of flight with us today." I wanted the jury to know that I agreed Hillard was a real expert, which he had done a fine job of proving. I continued, "You are the world's aerobatic champion. If I were a company designing a new aerobatic airplane, I certainly would have contacted you, talked to you about our new design, and hopefully retained you as a consultant."

"They did," he said.

"Great," I answered. I had no idea that he had been a consultant, but the next question was obvious: "So what did you write in your report?"

He stuttered. "Did . . . did I write a report?" He asked this question either to himself or to counsel. I couldn't tell which. Either way, it didn't look good.

"I don't know. Did you?" I answered.

"I don't remember," he said. At this point, he turned to counsel for help.

My next question was to Cooney. "Will you produce the report?"

It became obvious to everyone that they did have a report and hadn't produced it during the discovery process, which was a big mistake. Judges don't like that kind of "hide the weenie" stuff, and it looks bad in front of juries. Hillard didn't remember what he had written and clearly wanted to see it before he testified. He knew that I would use it to cross-examine him.

Montante was upset.

There was some back-and-forth. I got a little rougher. The defense denied that they had a report. I was quite sure that if they had hired Hillard as a consultant, they would have had him write a report. And anything that was written concerning the evaluation of the Aerobat would have been included in our request for production of documents.

After some back-and-forth, it turned out that they did have a report. At that point, Judge Montante stood up on his chair holding the big gavel with both hands. He bellowed, "Have you withheld evidence?"

Cooney was really hurt in the eyes of the jury. Not only did he have the report, but he had it with him or at least very close at hand.

You really can't guess what a jury thinks until the fat lady sings, but after this debacle, I was feeling pretty good. I was even more excited when I read the report that Hillard had written. The judge had discontinued the trial for an hour to permit me to do so.

In the report, Hillard had some criticisms of the plane followed by suggestions that had not been heeded. It was obvious now that he had been used as a rubber stamp. I would see more of this kind of behavior in future cases within the industry.

We could see the writing on the wall now. The defense had managed to anger the judge.

Bill Cooney then approached me. He said I didn't have much of a case, but he could call the claims manager and maybe talk him into getting our side a little money, like he was doing me a favor.

I wasn't interested. He seemed offended. Although there is always a risk, I felt it was worth going for the fence. I decided to leave to it to those women in the box rather than putt it out in the judge's chambers. It paid off! We won.

We had proven a design defect case. Shortly after the trial, the vertical tail was modified by Cessna, which effectively meant we had redesigned an airplane in the courtroom.

CHAPTER 5

The Rio Negro

*The stars seemed near enough to touch and
I never before have seen so many.
I always believed the lure of flying is the lure
of beauty, but I was sure of it that night.*

—*Amelia Earhart*

Amelia Earhart's Plane

He called it The Josephine Storm Door and Airplane Company and had handouts for the passengers that read, "Keep your feet off the damn seats."

Paul Valentino Esquire, which is how he referred to himself, was an attorney and had been an Air Force pilot. He was also a flamboyant, conservative, Italian Catholic who carried a firearm under his silk suit jacket and smoked cigarettes in a pearl cigarette holder. We both had been chairman of the aviation section of the Michigan State Bar Association. To my eye, we seemed to be the only two lawyers interested in representing victims and their surviving loved ones in airplane crash cases. He and I had both been suspicious of the NTSB as it often looked like they spent more effort protecting manufacturers and their insurers than anything else. The negative effect of this was the failure to learn from earlier design defects or simple mistakes, a suspicion that would become a certainty in the aftermath of Paul Valentino Esquire's plane crash.

I first met Paul about four years into my practice when I had the pleasure of trying a case against him in Oakland County, Michigan. The details of the case are hazy to me now, but those who watched the case in person referred to it as a contest between two egos vying to prove who knew the most about airplanes. I had met a match in this regard, and so had he.

We became friendly afterward. After all, we were both airplane guys and lawyers. However, he was most well-known for representing high-profile criminal cases. Several of his clients were organized crime figures with last names ending in vowels. He normally worked in Oakland County where the small town of Lake Orion was located.

On one instance, a mobster didn't pay Paul's bill. The man was subsequently arrested on a separate matter and held in the Oakland jail. Somehow, Paul learned that his criminal client had an expensive diamond ring with him in the holding cell. He filed a creditor's rights suit and served the county sheriff with a subpoena to take the mobster's diamond ring. When the mobster got wind of the subpoena, he swallowed the ring. Paul reacted by filing an injunctive type of lawsuit praying for relief. He was requesting that the sheriff have the ring removed at a designated nearby hospital. In law, courts referred to this as a prayer for equitable relief.

While the ring matter was still pending, Paul approached me to join him on a long trip in his airplane. I knew he owned an old antique airplane. He knew I had some experience in similar small transport airplanes like the Twin Beech or the D-18 and had some time in old tail draggers with radial engines.

It turned out that Paul's company, The Josephine Storm Door and Airplane Company, was the proud owner of a 1938 Lockheed 12AU Electra. The 12AU was the model flown by Amelia Earhart on her infamous attempted flight around the world. However, Paul's airplane had been modified with more modern engines.

In those days, the Pontiac Airport had become a hot spot for pilot-engineer-hobbyists, and upgrading and modifying older planes was popular. For my part, I had formed a corporation named the Paper Airplane Company, which purchased an old Aero Commander twin-engine aircraft for the purpose of performing some longitudinal stability tests for a pending case. When I was done, I intended to sell the old bird, but after hanging around the Pontiac Airport, I got the bug and decided to make some upgrades on it. I installed new engines which were slung under the wings, and then, being a very amateur spray-painter, created a major domestic issue when I ruined my wife's new car with overspray in the process of giving parts of the old Commander a new paint job in our garage.

As to the upgrades Paul had made on the Electra, he was having some trouble with the new Lycoming engines, a fact I wouldn't learn until later when we found the letter he had written to the manufacturer about a year before his fatal crash, on his legal stationery. Apparently, one engine had failed in flight, requiring an unscheduled emergency landing in Charleston, West Virginia. The question he asked the manufacturer was, "What will happen if both engines fail someday?"

Initially, our goal was to duplicate Amelia Earhart's flight around the world. However, we became concerned about the tremendous unrest in the Middle East. After talking about it for a while, I suggested we go to South America. He agreed, and we had our destination.

Part of the reason Paul agreed was that his late wife was from Maracaibo, Venezuela, and for some time, he had wanted to visit her parents. His wife had died from a gunshot wound during an attempted home robbery gone bad.

The both of us were also interested in seeing the Amazon River. So, after some planning, about two months later, we pointed the nose of the antique Lockheed southward and headed for the rainforests.

Based on today's standards, we had minimal navigation tools—certainly no GPS. We had a compass, a stopwatch, an automatic direction finder (ADF), and a variable omnidirectional receiver (VOR). The newest piece of technology we carried was the VOR receiver. Today, it is rapidly becoming an antique. At the time, it was only partially useful since once we crossed the north shore of the South American continent and entered the most dangerous part of the journey, there were very few VOR transmitters to help guide us.

To a large extent, we navigated by "dead reckoning," that is, compass heading, correcting for magnetic variation, true course, estimated ground speed, and time. However, the ADF was on a band that would pick up nondirectional beacons and AM radio broadcast stations if the power was great enough. This came to our rescue a few times.

I also had a cheap plastic sexton, but it was very difficult to get a good shot of the heavenly bodies from the cockpit through the wind screens. However, if the sun was out, I could find our location at noon on a clear day to within about a five-mile circle, which wasn't bad.

The Priest in the Amazon

We began the trip early one morning in the middle of June 1976, from runway 27L in Pontiac, Michigan. Our first stop was Fort Lauderdale, Florida (KFLL). We maintained visual flight rules so that we wouldn't be restricted in our maneuvers by air traffic control (ATC). We had planned to fully checkout the plane and its systems before being "coastout" of the southeast of U.S.

Since we had turbocharged engines, we planned to generally cruise at an altitude in the high teens. At those altitudes, we needed to breathe oxygen and had agreed that using cannulas (small tubes in the nostrils) would be more comfortable than oxygen masks for the many hours we planned to be aloft.

The 1,000 nautical miles to KFLL was uneventful, so we pressed on. After passing over the Bahamas and the Turks and Caicos archipelagos, we sighted Haiti. I was hoping to land at Cape Haitian, the location of the palace and the home of King, Baby Doc, but unfortunately, there was a wrecked airplane in the middle of the runway, and we couldn't land. Instead, we landed at Port-au-Prince.

It was an overwhelmingly poor place, even beyond expectations. There were poor, malnourished children in the streets.

We attempted to fuel late in the afternoon, but airport officials, all in badly-fitting uniforms, wouldn't let us near that side of the airport. As they spoke little English, it wasn't clear what the trouble was, but with heavy Cajun accents, they told us to leave the plane where it was with the brakes off and go to our hotel for the night.

"We will take care of it. We will take care of it." They insisted.

It was a little scary. At least we were allowed to lock the airplane. We did what they said. Returning in the morning, officials gave us a ride out to some obscure corner of the airport. Judging from the cockpit, it appeared that all seven fuel tanks had, in fact, been filled, but we could only guess as to what went into them. Throughout South America, we were concerned about getting clean fuel.

We had to go on faith that the fuel was the proper grade and clean. An error here might have been fatal since there were about eight hundred nautical miles of open water between Toussaint Louverture International Airport in Haiti and our first landfall on the north coast of South America at Cartagena, Colombia.

The engines fired up nicely despite our fears over the fuel, and we had no trouble as we taxied out to runway 28. That was a good sign. The only oddity was that on climb-out, I saw forklifts loading what was quite obviously bails of marijuana onto DC-6s. Now I understood why we were towed to the other side of the airport for fueling. And so it was during the 1970s in the Caribbean.

After landing in Cartagena, we went straight to the restaurant at our hotel. We were famished and immediately dug into a Colombian meal. I had been warned not to drink the water by the doctor in Michigan who administered our malaria shots and other medical protection for the potential diseases that might befall us in jungle country. So, I ordered Coca-Cola. How could I be hurt by bottled Coke? However, I poured it into a glass of ice. In one hour, I was so sick that I was afraid that I was not going to die. I remember lying on the floor of the *banyo* being attended by a Spanish-speaking doctor. At the time, I understood Spanish nada. After about a day and a half, I was able to move my lips, fingers, and toes. Paul showed up with a couple of travelers from Canada whom he had befriended while touring the nearby archaeological ruins. As it turned out, they joined us on the remainder of the adventure. Now there were four.

After about three days in Cartagena, we headed to the airport where we were informed that there was no fuel available for us. Based on information, we had reason to believe that the fuel they had was for preferred customers in large-transport cargo planes that paid large sums of cash. Doesn't take a lot of imagination. However, we were informed that there was fuel in Barranquilla, less than one hundred miles northeast, and we had adequate fuel to get there. Landing at Barranquilla, we were met by rather aggressive customs officials.

We immediately informed them that we had cleared customs in Cartagena. They replied, "We heard, but we wanted to show you something to think about." At that point, they escorted us to the back of a small building where we were shown a Cessna model 210 with an N registration, meaning it was from the United States. The airplane had several bullet holes in the windows and fuselage. The interior was splattered with blood. We got the message. We filled with fuel, filed a flight plan, and headed almost directly south at 18,500 feet, following the crest of the high country, landing in Bogotá. Our next intended stop was Manaus, Brazil. But a study of our planning charts showed that Bogotá to Manaus was right on the edge of the comfort zone of our fuel range.

According to Colombian law, it was necessary that we clear customs out of the country at an international airport. We spent an additional day in numerous government offices, obtaining permission to make a fuel stop in Villavicencio, Colombia, which was not a legal airport of entry or departure. With that done, we climbed out of Bogotá with some fancy official documents, stamped with a wax seal and ribbon. We believed these granted us permission to make a fuel stop in Villavicencio so we could have the extra fuel to make the trip comfortably to Manaus. That was what we believed.

Villavicencio Airport was a small unpaved field in the mountains. We landed and started to taxi toward what appeared to be a terminal of some type. All of the sudden, about six men in camouflaged suits armed with automatic weapons surrounded the airplane, pointing their guns at us. Paul was at the controls. He immediately gunned one engine and spun the plane around, knocking over a couple of the men, and headed back to the runway. We horsed our plane into the air again. I was sure we were going to be shot down. Yet no shots were fired. We were now in the air, over the mountains, and really tight on fuel to make it to Manaus, Brazil. There was not much between us and our destination but rain forest and jungle.

Before departing Bogotá, I looked at the forecasted winds aloft and estimated the pressure altitude for the best true airspeed. The forecasted winds were nil. However, a forecast is just that, an educated guess. Leaning the fuel to a mixture just about peak to give us the lowest fuel consumption, I concluded we would use just about every drop of fuel in all seven tanks. The charts showed a small unimproved landing strip about sixty miles short of Manaus. It could be an emergency bailout. So, we pressed on.

En route we talked about the pitfalls of ditching in the jungle.

Paul then pulled off a small strip of Velcro from the overhead and took out a 45-Magnum pistol and a small bottle of pills. He said, "This is my survival kit."

I responded, "What!?!"

He told me that the pills were Demerol and his plan was to take the pills and then shoot himself before the beast of the jungle ate him. I didn't know how to respond. I just filed it in my somewhat shocked little brain.

Our procedure was to run each of the seven fuel tanks empty before switching to the next, being careful not to suck air into the lines and to select the next tank in a sequence that would maintain balance.

At nine o'clock on the Fourth of July, we were on our last tank, a needle's width from empty, when I picked up a signal on 115.8 MHz from Manaus VOR indicating we had almost made it. As we landed on runway 11, first the left and then the right engine quit while taxiing in, and we needed to get towed to the FBO. That night, we celebrated the Fourth without a loud bang and without a need for the Demerol.

We arranged to hangar the airplane and then looked for lodging for the night. In the morning we looked for a guide and a boat to explore the Amazon and some of its headwaters. To our surprise, we found a priest, a reverend, or someone like that who was represented as knowing the waters in the area and who said that he serviced several of the native villages along the rivers. He volunteered to take us along and act as our guide. While he might have been a good guide with a sound knowledge of the Amazon and Rio Negro, he turned out not to be a good spiritual guide in the sense that I was raised.

At his instruction, we purchased quantities of fishhooks, cigarettes, pencils, paper, and bananas. The idea was to trade these items like currency to the natives for food. Together with the reverend, we boarded a large wooden outboard canoe and headed up the Rio Negro in search of adventure. Our guide warned us to watch for large Anaconda snakes. He said that we probably wouldn't see them, but we could smell their breath. They ate fish, he claimed, and if you caught a whiff of a fishy smell above the water near the shore, it was often a large snake in a tree. I never saw one but did experience the smell.

At the villages where we stopped, we found the people to be hospitable, and the food, if not gourmet, then palatable and often tasty. I thought it a big coup that we saw and ate a lot of piranhas after seeing the James Bond movies where piranhas finished off a human in minutes. The villages were right out of a *National Geographic* magazine, and the people were for the most part naked. We did find, however, that Right Reverend was taking a few liberties in the villages. The villages had just a few or no men, and it seemed that at each village, he went into a hut with one of the women. It looked like he really was servicing the villages. But no one seemed to mind.

We scouted around the Amazon and the headwaters for about a week. We played around with pink dolphins, caiman, freshwater stingrays, and even some very big snakes.

Next, we headed north to Venezuela. Paul had not yet seen his in-laws, and Eric and Adele, our Canadian friends, wanted to see Angel Falls. Angel Falls in Venezuela is the tallest, most uninterrupted waterfall in the world. I lowered the nose of the Lockheed and entered a descending spiral down to just a few hundred feet from the top of the falls. Spectacular! Then back to altitude and onto Maracaibo. We spent one night in this city known for its oil industry. The three of us went sightseeing while Paul visited his in-laws. The next night we spent in Caracas, in those days, one of the world's most romantic cities. We then put South America to our stern. On the way back north, we spent three great days scuba diving in Turks and Caicos. The reefs and wall diving treated us to many species of sea life and to the dramatic colors of many types of coral, including helmet fungi and other types of fan coral and more.

It was rather late at night when we landed at Pontiac, Michigan, without ever having to use the Demerol. It was Paul's rule to always lock the airplane in the hangar at night. He had his reasons. He called someone he trusted to come put the bird away, and we all left the airport.

That was the last time I saw Paul alive.

Double Engine Failure

The next morning, I got a call from Don Sommer. "The airplane is on fire, and your buddy's dead." He went on to say that it looks like he had suffered a double engine failure on takeoff and crashed into a cement plant. I was in shock. I had lost a good friend and I couldn't help but reflect on the thousands of miles of water and jungle that we had flown over, and this tragedy happened in our own backyard.

There were those who thought the engines failed because one of his enemies had the plane tampered with. In Paul's case, this was within the realm of possibility. He had scary clients and had made enemies. One of the first responders, who was a pilot and airplane mechanic, said that he had found at least one "B nut" loose in the fuel injection system while looking at the wreckage. But I would never be able to confirm this. The NTSB's behavior would ultimately bring me to another conclusion.

Within six hours, the NTSB had taken charge of the wreckage and the accident site. This was normal. Yet in this case, they moved in faster than usual.

The accident site was cordoned-off with yellow tape like a crime scene, and the wreckage was moved to a hangar at the Pontiac Airport. The NTSB's investigative team was initially made up of six or seven people: the investigator in charge, another NTSB employee, a representative of the FAA, and others who were employees of the engine manufacturer and/or, in fact, undercover employees of their product's liability insurance company, which might have to pay if there were any claims. In those days, this was the regular character of the NTSB investigative team and arguably the reason that the finding as to the cause of the crash was so often "pilot error." I was quite sure that the team was unusually concerned at the outset because

Valentino was an aggressive lawyer, and they were aware of the letter he had written to the engine manufacturer about the previous engine failure. The operative words must have been ringing in their heads, "What will I do someday when they both quit?" Additionally, they were likely aware that I was his friend and that his son had recently graduated from law school.

I immediately wrote to Lycoming, their insurance carrier, and the NTSB that I had been retained by the Valentino family and asked that their attorneys meet with me ASAP. The following day, all involved met at the Pontiac Airport terminal. There was the NTSB investigator in charge, a man from the FAA, two Lycoming representatives, and someone who identified himself as a representative from Lockheed. I was a bit skeptical as to whether some of these gentlemen were really as they represented. I was thinking certain ones were there to protect insurance company interests. At any rate, we reached an agreement that the wreckage would remain in the locked hangar where it was stored at the time, until after Paul's funeral. The funeral was the next day. We then would meet the following Monday to discuss further procedures. I was well aware that matters concerning the wreckage were controlled by the NTSB and took their word in trust. I might have been a tad young and naive.

The funeral was at 10:30 a.m. at a Catholic church just north of Lake Orion with a full Catholic mass. At about 1:30 p.m., everyone was leaving to gather at the cemetery, which was not far from the Pontiac Airport. As I left the service, I had an uneasy feeling in the pit of my stomach. I was concerned about the airplane wreckage. I decided to cruise by the airport on my way to the cemetery. I entered the airport perimeter on the north side where the hangar storing the wreckage was located. What I saw from a distance looked suspicious. As I got closer, I saw several vehicles and a twin-engine Beechcraft airplane. A cherry picker was actually loading Paul's engines into the Beechcraft. I also saw faces that I recognized from the meeting in which we agreed to leave the wreckage secured in the hangar until Monday. If only we were in the digital age and I could have photographed what I saw with my smartphone.

Needless to say, I never saw the engines again and never had a chance to examine them to determine why they both failed on takeoff. Although the NTSB had legal control and authority to deal with the wreckage, under Federal Regulatory Law, insurance interest was not permitted to be a party to NTSB investigation. I believed that it was the engine manufacturer's insurer, assisted by the NTSB and the FAA, who was behind the snatching of the engines during the funeral.

Therefore, I filed a claim against the NTSB and a lawsuit against Lycoming and their insurance company. I essentially accused them all of conspiring to destroy evidence. Eventually, the insurance company settled for a fair sum, and the NTSB gave lip service to cleaning up their act.

In my opinion, the reason the NTSB participates in these kinds of shenanigans is in part due to the fact that the Board is often light on technical expertise. The exception was that the Board did have a respectable metallurgical lab. Otherwise, they had to rely heavily on the manufacturer to assist in the investigations. This so often resulted in the published cause of the accident being diverted to "pilot error." It was akin to having the fox watch the henhouse. As a matter of fact, the real cause was often a combination of things. It might be a design defect, a manufacturing defect, poor maintenance, design-induced pilot error, or any combination of such.

The FAA, an agency of the Department of Transportation, is also usually involved in the investigation at some level. This agency has operational control of most every aspect of aviation. Their scope includes air traffic control, pilot issues, certification of new designs, and all rules pertaining to the operating of airplanes. Additionally, they have an extensive aeronautical engineering staff. The problem is the agency is given a statutory mandate to both promote the airline and manufacturing industry, and to police it. It was my experience that often the FAA had a problem handling this apparent conflict of interest.

In this case, it was quite clear that the government did not protect the interest of The Josephine Storm Door and Airplane Company, a.k.a. Mr. Paul Valentino Esquire's surviving family.

CHAPTER 6

Piston Twins

*Don't believe what your eyes are telling you.
All they know is limitations. Look with your
understanding. Find out what you already
know and you will see the way to fly.*

—Richard Bach, Jonathan Livingston Seagull

In spite of all we knew regarding the stability and control issues of light, twin-engine piston aircraft and the extreme difficulties these planes could encounter with one engine out, the crashes were usually blamed on pilot error. From my perspective, poor design was more often the cause, or a major contributing factor, than was commonly admitted. I wasn't just basing this belief on my own opinion derived from multi-engine training and engineering school; rather, I had to learn a lot about the characteristics of these aircraft when a friend of mine crashed and died in Colorado.

Tom Pierce lived at the Tri-County Airport in Erie, Colorado, in a home we lovingly referred to as the Dolly Parton house. The place consisted of two geodesic domes linked by a covered breezeway.

From the sky, it looked like . . . well, the joke was it looked like Dolly Parton's bosom.

Tri-County was more than an airport though. It was an airpark--a residential subdivision built in the late-1970s that allowed homeowners to taxi from the runway to their homes. These airparks were springing up around the country at the time.

Tom was a part-owner of the development and was actively engaged in growing its popularity. The year of his death, 1981, his efforts, among other things, included converting a Convair 990 jetliner, comparable in size to a Boeing 707 or a Douglas DC-8, into a restaurant at the airpark, which he called BJ Strawberries at the Convair. I had my fiftieth birthday party there. A band called the Fornicators played. Unfortunately, high interest rates and a moratorium on water stunted the restaurant, which eventually closed, and the Convair was broken up and carted away.

At Tom's house, one of the domes served as the residence, while the other was the hangar where he kept his personal twin-engine Cessna model 421. The 421 is a small pressurized, cabin-class aircraft often used for corporate and executive travel before small executive jets became vogue. The model had been FAA-certified by being added to the Cessna model 411 type certificate, which had been Cessna's first cabin-class piston twin-engine. It should be pointed out here that adding new models to existing type certificates is a trend we'll see throughout the book, which culminates finally in the catastrophe that is Boeing's 737 MAX.

It's also worth noting that the dangerous issues with Tom's plane were not unique to the Cessna 421 or the other Cessna 400 series. In fact, the 421 was better than many light twins in this regard; certainly, it was better than the Cessna model 411, which was a mean bird with an engine out. It's also not my intention to pick on Cessna in particular. The trouble was common to the basic configuration of these small twin-engine aircraft. There were several other light piston twins (light in this sense generally means under 12,500 lbs. maximum takeoff weight) with the same or similar problems. These included planes like the Beechcraft Travel Air, Beechcraft Baron, Piper Apache, Twin Commander, Aero-Star, and others. It was Cessna, in fact, that came up with a concept that helped mitigate one of the primary complications with twin-engine control when they added what they called a "blue line" speed to the airspeed indicator, which is explained in more detail below. It was also an addition that spread across the industry.

I was aware of light piston twin-engine airplanes and their bad accident rate before Tom's fatal crash. In fact, I had seen several crashes like his before. The first time was with a Beechcraft Travel Air that crashed in Livingston, Montana. This case was early in my career and had been referred to me by some of my co-workers back when I was at Continental. The crash was similar to Tom's in that the pilot had an engine failure on takeoff and was returning to the airfield. As his Beechcraft was turning onto final approach, it got a little slow, and when he added power on the good engine, the plane flipped over and crashed.

I had a general understanding of the handling problem with the light twins with one engine inoperative, but after Tom's crash, I decided to study this issue in detail and get the supporting data.

Crash at Tri-County Airpark

In Tom's case, he had just had one of the engines overhauled. It was a common requirement on piston engines to do an overhaul at 1,500 or 2,000 hours of use, so this was nothing out of the ordinary.

The trouble in this case was that the engine had been incorrectly reassembled. My notes as to the exact nature of the problem no longer exist. But it was a simple mistake.

That fatal day, Tom taxied out from the overhaul shop at Tri-County Airpark; the mechanic, having done the overhaul, was onboard with him. I'm surprised they even got as far as the departure end of the runway that day. It would have been better if they hadn't. As a result, their takeoff was catastrophic. Both men lost their lives.

Tom taxied onto runway 15, advanced the power levers and the propeller controls, and set the fuel mixture on the two engines. They accelerated to rotation speed, lifted off, and were climbing out when the freshly overhauled engine seized.

Tom was an experienced multi-engine pilot. He knew that he should push both power levers to the wall, establish a safe airspeed, identify the bad engine, and then feather its propeller (feathering changes the pitch of the propeller so as to line the blades up with the wind, decreasing the drag). Whatever he did, the airplane began turning to the northeast and then suddenly yawed, flipped over, went out of control, and crashed.

Certainly, it was in part the mechanic's fault as he had rebuilt the engine in such a way that it failed. But shouldn't the plane have been able to fly on one engine? The question remained: What brought it down? Was it pilot error, design defect, or a combination of both?

If it was pilot error, then had Tom feathered the wrong engine?

In this regard, we could tell by the propeller blades on the functioning engine that he hadn't made that mistake. So, what was it? Eyewitness testimony described gyrations of the airplane before the final impact consistent with a very particular loss-of-control scenario, which I will describe below. At this stage, there was very little empirical data to show why this loss of control with one engine inoperative was so predictable.

Flight Test

I knew we had to test some of these light twins with engines on the wings to have a full understanding of the stability and control issues. Also, I wished to document and display what was happening. But I certainly didn't have access to Boeing's test facilities at this time. In fact, I didn't have a facility at all. But as it turned out, after Tom's death, his wife was in no shape to run the airport, and she didn't wish to live in the house with the twin domes anymore. She asked my partners if we could run the airport for a while.

When that happened, I got to thinking the Erie airport would make a great test base for instrumenting and test flying a few general aviation airplanes. The Dolly Parton house was no longer occupied. That could be our test facility.

Trying to measure in-flight parameters and collect data was one of my favorite projects back at Boeing. I love to design what we called transducers, which is a way to take a mechanical force, displacement, velocity, acceleration, a temperature, or other such quantity and turn it into an electrical signal to be stored, transmitted, and analyzed. With this airport suddenly available for our use, I had an opportunity to do something I greatly missed after leaving Boeing,

Not only did we use the airport for this, a good friend and engineering pilot rented Tom's house, which Tom's wife no longer wanted to occupy. The Dolly Parton house gave us a great base of operations. Shortly thereafter, the house became available again. I decided to move in with my two youngest kids. It was a good house for kids as well, and I brought my children there to live on the airport and near my work. However, my ex-wife didn't like the idea as much as I did. She saw children living on an airport and flying in small airplanes as dangerous and threatened to file for an injunction to prevent the kids from flying in general aviation airplanes. I did understand her point. Being a lawyer in our firm, she was more aware than most about general aviation accidents, but for the short term, I pressed on. After all, I had a runway and a hangar in my backyard.

The first project was to acquire a Cessna 421 for the purpose of performing some flight tests. I found one that had a serial number close to the one in which Tom Pierce was killed. Once I had my hands on the Cessna, we immediately set about designing and installing instrumentation so we could produce data.

One of my biggest criticisms of Cessna was their lack of any hard data. While during the certification process, they should have been required to present adequate data to the FAA. In our lawsuit, we requested the certification data pursuant to the Colorado Rules of Civil Procedure, and to our surprise, what they had was pathetic.

What I would consider essential data for finalizing the design and certification of this piston twin was missing in both the regulatory data we received from the FAA and the data produced as discovery pursuant to the court rules. Either it was being hidden or they didn't have it, though I suspected they didn't have it. A fact that would prove embarrassing for them in a courtroom. In very short order, we were going to know more about their airplane than they did.

For the purposes of my analysis, the missing data included (1) the aerodynamic information necessary to determine vertical tail power available under various engine inoperative flight conditions, (2) the geometric information necessary to calculate the conservation of momentum in the entry to a spin, and (3) the actual thrust developed by the engines under various conditions.

I was able to accomplish item 2 by measuring the exemplar airplane and doing the appropriate calculations. Items 1 and 3 required instrumenting and flying the airplane. By doing so, we were able to get a good look at the aerodynamic data on the vertical tail by measuring the pressure profile of its aerodynamic surfaces using a series of strategically installed pressure transducers.

For item 3, thrust developed by the engine, we installed load cells on the propeller shafts and used slip rings. The slip rings allowed us to pass an electric current from the rotating shaft to a stationary circuit to collect data. With the instrumentation installed, we did extensive flight tests with one engine at zero thrust as well with propellers feathered and windmilling (that is, the relative wind turning the propeller). Additionally, we recorded data with different configurations of landing gear, flaps, and changes in center of gravity. We also looked at side slips, skids, and propeller wash.

What's the Matter with the Piston Twins?

We used the data collected in these tests at the Tri-County Airpark as demonstrative evidence in the lawsuit against Cessna. The case was in state court in the City and County of Denver. The claims against the maintenance company were obvious. The claim against Cessna was a design defect, alleging that the engine-out controllability was inadequate and misrepresented by the manufacturer.

It took about two years to prepare the Pierce case for trial. From the beginning, I was asking myself the question: If this type of platform is so tricky to fly, then why haven't engineers looked at it more closely? Why wasn't there better empirical data on these machines? As far as we could tell from the courtroom, we were the only people who ever bothered to extensively test these aircraft and record inflight data, a neglect that helped our law practice of course, but was also frightening when you consider how many people were at risk in these aircraft over the years.

By trial, we were well-prepared. In fact, it seemed that we knew considerably more about the aerodynamics of the airplane than the manufacturer did. This data proved a great deal about the dangers in the classic piston twin aircraft that would apply to just about any case that might cross my desk in the future. The data largely included aerodynamic data that the companies and even the FAA didn't have. It enabled us to settle the case for Mrs. Pierce and also allowed us to urge design improvements in the industry that made planes safer, which had been my goal.

As I understood going into the case, which our tests verified, the root of the problem was the location of the engines, the area and shape of the vertical tail, and the distribution of weight (i.e., fuel tanks, engines, etc.). All the twins, with the exception of the Cessna 337 Skymaster and the Adams aircraft prototype, had the engines mounted out on the wings. What this meant was that in the case of an engine failure, the operating engine, together with the drag of the inoperative one, would cause an asymmetric thrust that wanted to turn the plane in the direction of the failed engine, which often proved deadly. Under so many flight conditions, there was insufficient tail power to maintain control with one engine inoperative.

Loss of control in twin-engine airplanes with one engine inoperative is most often an issue of Vmc (velocity minimum control). V_{mc} is the speed below which there is insufficient tail power and control of adverse drag to maintain control when one engine is out.

The classic twins controlled asymmetric thrust with the vertical tail and rudder. Simple enough, but keeping the plane in flight, especially at or near takeoff and landing speeds, is tricky. Aeronautical engineers know that the ability to keep a plane from going out of control in the yaw axis is a function of "tail power." This is a function of the distance from the aerodynamic center of the airplane to the aerodynamic center of the surfaces of the tail, which works like a torque wrench. The weight distribution comes into play due to the conservation of angular and linear momentum, wherein those heavy things, like engines and wingtip fuel tanks, when in motion, want to continue on their path whether curved or straight. And while the tail power works to stop a spinning airplane, momentum makes it more difficult. Tail power is the fundamental struggle in all classic twin-engine aircraft, but it's especially tricky in twin piston-engine aircraft because the engines are very heavy for the power they can develop, and in airplane design, weight is paramount.

As mentioned above, V_{mc} is the speed below which there is not enough tail power to counter the effects of the asymmetric thrust caused by the functioning engine. The speed is also a published airspeed limitation and differs from model-to-model. But, by publishing this speed as manufacturers did, one might think that the number was certain and fixed—like the number of inches in a foot. However, it is not. Although V_{mc} was most often published as a single number, it can vary substantially based on a variety of factors: sideslip, propeller wash, vertical tail lift characteristics, the actual thrust on the operating engine, bank angle, and other more subtle issues. Although V_{mc} was used in multi-engine training for many years, at some point, Cessna decided that reliance on the published V_{mc} was dangerous. Thus, they added a somewhat arbitrary fudge factor and called it safe single-engine speed. This they put on the airspeed indicator as a blue-line.

Cessna's "blue-line" speed, as it came to be known, had been the number used for several years as the engine-out training for all brands—whether a Cessna or not. This "blue-line" speed is a higher number and generally equal to the best rate of climb speed, known as Vy.

After the publishing of the blue-line speed, instructors would say, "If you lose an engine on takeoff, lower the nose and go for the blue-line. This speed is likely to provide more controllability, but not always."

All multi-engine pilots are trained to fly with one engine inoperative under various modes of flight, including takeoff, cruise, and landing. Takeoff is probably the most difficult with one engine inoperative because the plane is at maximum power, which results in the maximum asymmetric thrust while at the same time the plane is at a low airspeed and near stall and Vmc speeds.

Though they train for such eventualities, real-life events are seldom like training. For one, in training, the student is anticipating a failure. Whereas in real life, everything happens so fast, and it takes some time to mentally sort out the problem, making the situation more difficult to understand. It's often not clear which engine has failed. It's possible both engines are acting up from such things as contaminated fuel or induction of ice. Therefore, not only does the one engine inoperative scenario have a remedy that is itself challenging, but the pilot must diagnose the problem, and time is short.

I personally found landing with an engine out challenging and different from the training, which required an unorthodox remedy in my case.

Many years ago, I was out practicing single-engine flight with my twin-engine Shrike Commander, a high-wing airplane with two engines mounted on each wing with a very low-slung fuselage. I had hung new factory-rebuilt engines on the bird and painted the airplane myself. The landing gear on the Shrike extended out of the engine nacelles and was larger than that on most light twins. The long legs made the plane look somewhat like a big bug when the wheels were out.

That day, I had shut down one engine and feathered the propeller to practice flying on one engine. Unfortunately, when it came time to restart the out engine, it wouldn't start. After several attempts, I started to look for a place to make a single-engine landing.

When I had found a suitable airport with a long runway and was given a clearance to land, I lined up for my final approach. At about five miles out, I extended some flaps and the landing gear. But in short order, I realized that with the gear and flaps down, I wasn't going to make it to the runway with this additional drag. I then retracted the landing gear, which allowed me to make it over the perimeter fence. Since I didn't have time to re-extend the gear, I was forced to land wheels up on the plane's belly. I put it on the grass next to the runway.

It was fortunate that the Commander had a high wing and a fuselage that was conducive to such a landing. I was very lucky and did practically no damage to the Shrike. But if I hadn't put the landing gear back up, we would have crashed.

I mention this example to show how my thinking on this type of plane had changed from owning one to believing over the course of time that the negatives outweighed the positives. I can't date when I began to feel this way about light twin-piston aircraft because it was a development over time, but Tom's case forced me to look into the problem more deeply and to come to a conclusion.

No one plans to crash, of course. However, an obvious reason you buy a twin-engine airplane is to cover yourself for the day when an engine fails in flight. But there is a legitimate case to be made that most pilots would do better with an engine failure in a single-engine airplane than in a light twin. Sadly, however, a large percentage of the fatal accidents in twins happened during training. The unfortunate fact is, under the more critical modes of flight, when one engine fails on a twin, the plane loses about 80 percent of its ability to fly. The pilots are then left with a mean beast on their hands, which is why it is often said that the second engine merely takes you to the scene of the crash and makes a louder noise.

In general, all these light-piston twin aircraft (Beechcraft, Piper, Cessna, Aero Commander, and possibly Aerostar) had similar V_{mc} problems. Some were better, and others worse, but all suffered from the same challenge to some extent. In addition to the handling issues with one engine inoperative, piston engines use gasoline as compared to jet fuel or kerosene, used by diesels, turbo props, and jets. Gasoline is much more volatile and a far greater fire hazard.

Among the piston twins, the Piper Aztec was probably the safest and least hazardous with an engine out. It had better handling characteristics but gave up performance. Whereas other twin pistons cruised at about 200 MPH, the Aztec's cruising speed was around 160 MPH. By comparison, the stall speeds were lower, which translated, among other things, to a lower landing and takeoff speed. Additionally, its stall characteristics were more docile. The predecessor to the Aztec was the Piper Apache. This was affectionately referred to as the "half-ass tech," which was smaller and had smaller engines.

Comparing a piston engine to a turbo-prop, also known as a jet-prop, the turbo-prop engines will typically weigh about one-fourth the weight of a piston engine of the same horsepower. The heavier engines result in more angular momentum, which is a negative in a spin or in spin recovery. Additionally, during an engine failure event, it is imperative that the propeller be feathered immediately after the engine fails. If not feathered, the propeller on the failed engine will windmill (wind flowing over the airplane will keep turning the propeller on the dead engine), causing tremendous drag and also spoiling the air over the tail. On many turbo-prop twins, the propellers auto-feather, but on the piston twins, the pilot has to manually feather the propeller, which can be another problem in itself. A cause we had ruled on in Tom Pierce's case.

As with most things, there was an exception. The piston twin that didn't have these dangerous issues was known as the Cessna Skymaster, but this plane had an entirely different configuration and had been designed with the engines on the front and back of the fuselage, as opposed to out on the wings, a concept known as in-line thrust or centerline thrust. If a pilot had been trained in a Skymaster, the license was limited to such an airplane. Flying other multi-engine aircraft required additional training.

Skymasters were safer to fly. However, the joke around airports was that Skymasters were sissy airplanes and that the pilots who flew them should have to wear Mickey Mouse ears.

I guess you were considered cool if you could fly a more dangerous airplane. Like *Top Gun*, you had to be willing to fly on the edge of the envelope, even if you were just making a business trip. This mentality, which was shot throughout the industry and among pilots, explains in part why pilots and owners tolerated more dangerous aircraft.

Aside from the reputation that it was only flown by pilots who didn't have the "right stuff," the Skymaster was at least an attempt to make a safer twin-engine piston-powered airplane.

I owned a few of them. One drawback was that you couldn't see the rear engine from the cockpit. This feature came into play once when I was landing on Runway 33 at Detroit City Airport. We had a rear engine fire and didn't even know it until we had landed and were rolling out. People on the ground kept waving and pointing at us. Whereas in a conventional piston twin, we might have seen the fire and shut the engine down while we were at a speed too low to have control. Then we would have had an airplane with very bad manners that really wanted to spin toward the inoperative engine.

Bar Harbor and the Fox Watching the Henhouse

We tried a series of light twin cases during the 1980s, and with the empirical data we had gathered from the Pierce case, we were able to bring about some design changes, though not enough to satisfy my goal. In my view, the light piston twins are still a very marginal platform.

Another aspect of the platform's impediment, which came up in the Bar Harbor case, was the necessity of feathering the propellers in the event of an engine failure. Under most circumstances, it was necessary to feather the propeller on the bad engine to stay in the air. This was also the standard training technique. But the technique assumes the feathering mechanism will work when an engine becomes inoperative. What happens if it doesn't? The answer is you have one mean plane to fly, a plane that wants to turn into the inoperative engine, fall below Vmc speed, and go out of control.

We had the opportunity to try just such a case. The result would further put both Cessna and the FAA in the hot seat.

By now it was the mid-1980s, I had tried several light twin-engine cases by this time, but this particular Cessna 400 crash sticks out in my mind. The plane was being operated as an air-taxi service and crashed on approach to the Bar Harbor Airport in Trenton, Maine.

Like so many light-twin accidents, what the pilots actually encountered was not like the typical training scenario. In this case, the propeller governor shaft broke, causing the propeller pitch angle to go haywire while the plane was on final approach. Apparently, the crew advanced the power on the good engine while at low airspeed, the prop wouldn't feather on the bad engine, and the aircraft did the classical Vmc out-of-control roll. All aboard were killed. Now this was a different scenario from a simple engine failure, but nevertheless, the flight crew were faced with the same light twin-engine design issues, and all were killed.

I was brought into the case by a bright local plaintiff's attorney whose practice was in Bangor, Maine. He told me that he heard about our flight testing on light twin-engine airplanes and wondered whether we had any data on the flight characteristics with one engine inoperative that could help. He had come to the right place.

We met not long after and talked about our data and analysis. He then asked if I would be willing to try the case, which I was. His plan was to file a motion in federal court for the District of Maine to have me admitted *pro hac vice* for this one occasion. The court granted the motion, and I entered my appearance.

We started jury selection on a cold and snowy winter morning in downtown Bangor. I'll never forget trudging through the snow from my lodgings at the Phoenix Inn to the federal courthouse carrying large cases of documents, including legal pleadings, engineering drawings, and flight test data.

That morning, while in the shower, I was thinking: *What gems did I have that I want to plant in the jury's mind right from the very beginning?* In my mind, people will tend to remember the first things they hear or see, and maybe the last things, more than what might go on in the middle of a trial. The concept is referred to as primacy and recency. I remembered from their pleadings that they were going to raise the defense known as federal preemption. That is, because the airplane was certified by the FAA, it is assumed to be airworthy and a good design and cannot be found defective by a court or jury. I knew that all aircraft were legally required to have an FAA airworthiness certificate on board. During the wreckage inspection of the airplane, I had looked at its airworthiness certificate. It was of the proper format but was signed by a Cessna employee on behalf of the FAA. Wasn't this a classic case of the fox watching the henhouse? Maybe the jury should hear this in the opening statement or even during jury selection?

Bar Harbor Airlines served the route from Bangor to Bar Harbor. What this meant in our case was that we needed a couple of days to finish the jury selection because so many people on the jury array knew someone who had lost a loved one in the crash.

It was on the third day that I made an opening statement. Now in an opening statement, it is objectionable to argue the case as the stated purpose of such a statement is to tell the jury what the proofs are going to show. However, most good trial lawyers will generally sneak in a little argument on the way. If that draws an objection, then the objection itself can be used advantageously. For example, the lawyer making the opening statement might reply to the objection, "Please don't interrupt me while I'm talking to these folks." Jury trials are mostly about impressions and believability, and small interactions like this can go a long way to casting the other side in a negative light. I used this technique quite often. In many ways, good trial lawyers know how to go right up to the line and sometimes to cross it. If handled well, even the penalties can be used to your advantage.

Another technique that served me well was to call a hostile witness first. In this case, the witness I was planning on calling first was an executive engineer for the Cessna Airplane Company. I told the jury that he wasn't on the side of the plaintiff, that is, those who had lost their loved ones. Often, I would tell a jury in the opening statement, "The first witness that you will hear will be a man who wants my clients to lose this case. But he will be under oath. He will be someone who probably knows more about this airplane than most, and although he doesn't want to, he will admit to the defect in the product that gives rise to this lawsuit." Most lawyers believed that calling an adverse witness in your own case is risky and foolish. I believed that it worked well because the rules generally allow cross-examination of an adverse witness. That is, leading questions can be used. Leading questions allow putting the answer in the question. For example, "Isn't it true that the crash in this case is because the windshield on this Learjet was not strong enough to withstand hitting the bird?" You have said that in the opening, and now, right after the opening, you're saying it again. Additionally, he or she can't deny it. The best they can do is give some excuse. Also, there are many questions where the answer can't hurt your case no matter what it is. An example is, "What is the maximum allowable takeoff weight of this plane, or what is the wingspan?" If the witness gets it correct, that's good information for you to use as a check on your own expert witness, so your witness won't make a mistake. If he or she gets it wrong, it hurts them. Because of their position in the company, they should know the right answer.

I explained in my opening statement that my first witness "doesn't want them to win this case. But I believe he's an honest man, and regardless of his obvious loyalty to the company, he will tell the truth after he takes an oath. Listen carefully!" I also pointed out his obvious conflict of interest. "You'll also see that he wears two hats. He has a built-in conflict of interest because he is expected to be loyal to the company—but he's also been designated by the FAA to oversee the airplane design and certify that the airplanes are in compliance with FAA-published design and build standards. You'll hear that he actually signed the 'airworthiness certificate' for the airplane that crashed that dark rainy night, attempting to land at the Bar Harbor Airport."

After the plaintiff's opening statement, I called Mr. Wells of the Cessna Airplane Company.

"Mr. Wells, please step forward and be sworn. In addition, the plaintiff will ask the court to designate this gentleman as a hostile witness: he is a management employee of an adverse party."

With the technique of using leading questions, I could put in the lion's share of our case with a witness employed by the defendant, and he would have to agree with what was true or make the case that my facts were wrong. Of course, it helped that I had a long history of engineering and piloting.

After the witness was sworn, I proceeded to thank him for coming all the way from Wichita to help the jury figure out what happened that fateful night. Next, I asked, "Mr. Wells, how much does the Model 402A weigh when it is loaded to its maximum takeoff weight?"

"I'm not sure. I would have to look it up."

Next, "What is the horsepower of the engines on the Model 402A?" And, "What is the order of magnitude of the thrust of those engines at the normal cruise altitude?"

He responded, "I think the horsepower is about 350, and the thrust would have to be calculated."

Next, "Mr. Wells, isn't it true that if you knew the thrust and the distance from the aerodynamic center of the airplane, you could calculate the tail power required?"

Moving on, I would ask him, "Isn't it true that your company published Vmc as a constant number when it is in fact a variable?"

My aim with these questions was to use Mr. Wells to lay a foundation for the flight test data we had acquired during testing at the Dolly Parton hangar. Next, I had Mr. Wells admit that the driveshaft on the propeller governor had broken. While I had him on the stand, I showed him the airworthiness certificate for the subject airplane. He agreed that he had signed the certificate, although it was probably a stamped signature.

Not only had I established many of the case's facts from the mouth of a hostile and presumably "expert" witness, I had now also established that a Cessna employee was signing the certificate on behalf of the FAA. This was a nice way to show the court and the jury the conflict of interest. My intended message was that the regulated were acting as the regulator and signing off on a poor design.

The result was that we went on to prove our point concerning the plane's design and win a major victory in Maine. More important than the victory for our law firm, it was becoming more and more difficult for the manufacturers to get away with producing poorly-designed planes and simply falling back on the argument that either the planes had been in service for some time or that the FAA had signed off on the design. Defective design was defective design, period; juries could see it.

At the design criteria stage of any design project, the engineers must look at potential failures and the foreseeable use and mis-use of the product.

In the case of piston twins, the manufacturers know that people purchase twins to get an extra margin of safety. The impression in the public's mind is that the additional engine will get them back on the ground safely in the event of engine failure. However, it is so often not the case. The designers also know that these twins will regularly be used for multi-engine training. In the training process, we have seen many fatal accidents. Instructors must operate very close to the edges of the envelope, where these light twins have some very bad manners.

Because piston twins were a fixture of the airplane industry with known limitations, and exceptional skill was required with one engine inoperative, it was common for pilots and flight instructors to jump to the conclusion that pilot error was the true cause of a light twin crash when it underwent an uncontrollable Vmc gyration. But years of wind-tunnel and flight testing, university and military schools on airplane performance and stability and control, power plant design, and accident investigation have given me a different view. These light piston twins are a dangerous platform. It doesn't make it safer that many pilots have landed with an engine out. The numbers of fatal crashes are simply too high on this platform.

Today you'll find fewer and fewer light twins powered by gasoline piston engines in service in the United States. In part this is because of the many lawsuits.

I used to wonder where they all had gone, but as I flew more regularly to the Caribbean Islands and South America, I've found these old piston twins operating in many third world countries where the regulations and courts are less stringent.

Yet all this knowledge notwithstanding, I have owned several light piston twins and flown many more owned by others. I've learned a lot, accepted the risk a lot, but regularly stayed away from the corner of the flight envelope, didn't always rely on the manufacturer's numbers, and been lucky a lot. After sixty years of flying, I still climb the skies and remain a happy birdman.

CHAPTER 7

Kenneally

If you want to find out the secrets of the Universe, think in terms of energy, frequency, and vibration.

—*Nikola Tesla*

Leonard Kenneally, a United Airlines Boeing 727 captain, had flown his private single-engine Cessna, model 210, to the four corners area of southwest Colorado from Longmont, Colorado, to check out potential campsites. It was midafternoon when he was returning to the front range of the Rockies. He was in cruise flight on the leeward side of the Sangre de Cristo mountain range when his plane started to shake violently and porpoise. He had to know that he was losing control. We can only imagine the terror.

A camper heard an airplane with an unusual engine noise. She looked up and saw a broken airplane coming straight down into the mountains; part of its wing was missing. A five-foot section of the left wing was found about a half mile from the fatal crash site. Captain Kenneally was the only one onboard.

My office represented Shirley Kenneally, Leonard's wife. A wrongful death case was filed in district court for the City and County of Denver, Colorado, against Cessna Aircraft Company, the designers and manufacturer of the airplane, and Judson Flying Service, which had been involved in the maintenance and/or inspection of the plane.

It was a product liability case against Cessna. The claim was defective design of the airplane structure. Specifically, we claimed that the airframe was prone to structural dynamic instability, known as flutter, which could cause an in-flight structural dynamic failure under normal and foreseeable flight conditions. In this case, the model 210 was flying in turbulence over the Rocky Mountains, on a July afternoon, by a highly-trained professional pilot; the idea of pilot error seemed a bit of a stretch.

However, the NTSB concluded that the "probable cause" of the in-flight structural breakup was the pilot flying in clear air turbulence at an airspeed higher than V_A (maneuvering speed) or, in other words, pilot error. The NTSB investigative team consisted of an employee of the NTSB with little aeronautical knowledge, a representative of Cessna, and a representative of the defendant Judson Flying Service. But there was nobody on this team representing the deceased pilot. More often than not, the NTSB will find "pilot error" in a general aviation case, following a rather limited and cursory investigation, assisted by parties whose products might be the cause of the crash.

So often, after we have completed our accident reconstruction, test, and analysis, we disagreed with the "probable cause" published by the National Transportation Safety Board. Additionally, we would often come to court with more flight test data and a more complete and detailed engineering analysis than the defendant manufacturer.

In general aviation, the findings of the NTSB are more often than not "pilot error." Are pilots just poorly trained? Does one have to be a "top gun or a "superhero" to fly airplanes? Or is there a lot of design-induced pilot error? The marketing material depicts families—Mom, Dad, and the kids—going on vacation in the family airplane. We see advertising in flying magazines depicting doctors, bankers, and lawyers taking their friends on vacations to the Bahamas or other vacation spots reachable only by general aviation airplanes. Are general aviation private airplanes designed to be safely flown by the people to whom they are marketed? After all, these private pilots are usually licensed by the FAA.

In fact, in the Kenneally case, the pilot was a highly-trained commercial jet airline pilot who was flying a private general aviation airplane.

Although the NTSB's "probable cause" statement is part of an official record published by the federal government, it is not admissible in court. There is a federal statute prohibiting its admissibility in a civil trial. Notwithstanding this statute, much of the NTSB's factual report does come into evidence in civil trials involving airplane crashes. Many times, the factual part of the NTSB report implies or infers "pilot error." In this regard, trial lawyers must be careful.

Airplane in-flight structural failures are generally a disaster, without survivors. They can range from the Kenneally Cessna model 210 in this chapter, which claimed one life, to the in-flight structural failure of the empennage of American Flight 587, which took the lives of 260 people. In both cases, these in-flight structural breakups were blamed on the pilot. In neither case did the investigative team include anyone representing the pilots. In both of these examples, when the facts were correctly developed and analyzed, it was proven that defective design was most likely the "probable cause."

Although airplanes can breakup because of weather, mid-air collisions, or the acts of terrorists, here I will talk about those in-flight breakups caused by overloaded structure resulting from poor design. When I use the words *loaded* or *overloaded*, I am talking about forces, both static or dynamic (i.e., steady forces or those caused by motion). It is the duty of the designer to design for the foreseeable loads that will be experienced in the operation of an airplane. The minimal standards for design of airplane structures are set forth in Section 14 of the United States Code of Federal Regulations. Among these standards is the requirement for a safety factor of 1.5, meaning that it's fifty percent stronger than its breaking strength. Compared to building structures, bridges, etc., this is a very small safety factor. Buildings and bridges don't have to fly, so weight isn't so important. In civil engineering, it is not unusual to see safety factors of 3 plus. Because of the small safety factor used in designing aircraft structures, load analysis and structural integrity are extremely critical.

Airplanes may be subjected to a wide variety of loading conditions during flight. Among such things are variations in speed, flight control inputs and resulting maneuvers, power plant weight and thrust, and the flight environment, both standard and extreme, such as gust and turbulence.

The proper architecture for the structure and the proper choice of materials are imperative in the airplane design process. The proper test and analysis are critical in the proof of design process. In chapter 10, you will hear about a fatal choice of an inappropriate material. Here I talk about a particular aspect of airplane structural architecture. The structural architecture will substantially determine the integrity of the airframe. This is particularly true with regard to the structural dynamics concept known as aeroelasticity and aerodynamic flight flutter.

The best analogy that I can offer is a non-aviation incident. Back in 1940, the Tacoma Narrows Bridge in the state of Washington, a suspension bridge, which spanned the strait of Puget Sound between Tacoma and the Kitsap Peninsula, was totally destroyed by an unstable structural dynamic event. The bridge collapsed into the Narrows as a result of aeroelastic flutter as a result of a sympathetic vibration. The oscillations became divergent after being triggered by the wind. This particular unstable oscillatory event had a lasting effect on engineering and science.

Back at Boeing, flight flutter was an issue for which we tested very early in the flight testing of a new model. It is very important to know early in the process if a new model was structurally dynamically stable and would not tear itself apart under predictable modes of flight. Test pilots and crews receive hazardous duty pay because flutter testing could be very dangerous.

Flutter, as the term means when applied to an airplane in flight, refers to a dynamic instability of an aerodynamic structure such as a wing, tail, or stabilizer. It can also apply to a control surface such as a rudder or elevator. Such structures are elastic in nature because when moved or stretched, they want to return to their original state of balance or position. The concept is analogous to a rubber band when stretched or a pendulum moved from its resting position. When such structures are moved or excited, they can start to oscillate. The oscillatory movement is akin to a low-frequency vibration. In the case of aerodynamic flutter, it will generally be in a frequency range less than 20 cycles per second or 20 Hz. The forces acting on an oscillating component are the aerodynamic forces of the airflow, the elastic forces of the structure trying to return it to its original state, and the inertia that wants it to remain in motion once it starts to oscillate.

In an airplane, it is crucial that, when excited, the oscillation of the structure dampens or ceases within very few cycles. When excited by some force, such as an aerodynamic input, like a change in lift or some random force such as turbulence, it could be a disaster if the oscillation goes divergent and fails to dampen.

At Boeing, flight testing for structural dynamics was flown with a minimum crew and, if possible, with an escape mechanism and parachutes. On the ground, there was a telemetering room that receives data from the test airplane remotely using wireless transfer of data. Structural dynamic engineers in the telemetry room were in constant radio contact. The test crew would start at a relatively low airspeed and low Mach number and attempt to excite the oscillation and wing or control surface. The excitation was done by an abrupt control input or some other method. One example that I remember was attaching shotgun shells to the wing and firing them remotely. After the excitation, the engineers would plot the data, do an analysis, and decide whether it was safe to clear the test aircraft to a high airspeed for another excitation. The test was accomplished at increasing airspeeds, a few knots at a time up to, and a hair over, the maximum allowable design airspeed. The reason the speed was a factor is that the aerodynamic forces would change with airspeed and Mach number. If the oscillations were acceptably dampened up to the maximum allowable airspeed and Mach number, the plane was considered flutter-cleared.

I was fortunate enough as a young engineer to be instructed on doing the structural dynamic analysis in the telemetering room and to communicate with the test crew. This learning process was fun and exciting.

One night during the Kenneally trial, I was sitting in my kitchen table in Boulder, Colorado, wondering how I could best get the jury to understand the flutter concept and the dampening issue. I happened to look over at knife rack sitting on the counter. I walked over and pulled out the longest butcher knife. Holding the handle firmly down on the countertop with my left hand, I plunked the tip of the knife with my right hand. The blade oscillated about three times; each oscillation had a smaller amplitude until it dampened to a standstill. I said to myself, "This would be great demonstrative evidence to get my point across to the jury tomorrow." I put the knife in my briefcase for use the next day in court.

The next morning, we were back in court with old Judge Kingsley presiding. We were in the defense part of the case, and Cessna had just finished the direct examination of their star expert, Dr. Kollman. The defense lawyer said, "Your witness." On that cue, I reached in my briefcase and pulled out the butcher knife and said, "Judge, may I approach the witness." Old Judge Kingsley laughed and said, "Okay, but be very careful." I replicated the routine that I had done the night before on the kitchen countertop. It seemed that the jury understood the idea of dampening an oscillating structure.

Captain Kenneally's airplane lost a portion of the left wing in flight that fateful July afternoon, not because of wing flutter but because of control flutter of the elevator on the empennage of his single-engine airplane. This can happen when a control surface is not properly balanced about its hinge line. That was what happened here. The imbalance on the airplane at issue was caused by two things: a trim control actuator that was attached to the elevator surface and some foam material that had been installed as a stiffener in the elevator structure.

Turbulence is a regular condition experienced over the Rocky Mountains on a summer afternoon. It was likely that turbulence is what excited the flutter of Captain Kenneally's elevator. The elevator oscillations then caused porpoising and ultimately loss of control.

The wing structure would have failed because of forces experienced while the plane was tumbling out of control.

Kenneally v. Cessna was a hard-fought trial. I tried this case with my partner Bruce Lampert, a naval aviator who had become a great trial lawyer. The judge said that when Lampert speaks, the building shakes, and the jury weeps.

After approximately two weeks of trial, a jury found that the cause of the fatal crash was a defect in the design of the airframe, which excited an unstable divergent structural dynamic condition known as flight flutter, which tore the airplane apart in-flight. The jury heard the testimony of several aeronautical experts: an engineer specializing in accident reconstruction who had examined many documents and conducted experiments and lab analysis on the actual structural parts from the wreckage, and two professors of aeronautical engineering with PhDs. This jury also examined many photographs and watched some convincing demonstrative evidence.

CHAPTER 8

Learjet

I've topped the wind-swept heights with easy grace
Where never lark, or ever eagle flew --

"High Flight" by John Gillespie Magee

It seems that no matter how many cases you've tried, there is always an adrenaline rush when the trial begins.

The bailiff bellowed, "Hear ye, hear ye! The United States District Court for the Eastern District of Michigan is called to order."

We were now underway.

The judge called, "The case of the personal representative of Donald Treu, deceased, versus the United States. Please state your appearances."

I stood. "Richard Schaden for the plaintiff, Judge."

In a rather harsh voice, the judge responded, "It's Your Honor, counsel!"

I had been mentored by an old civil rights lawyer. His name was Harry. He firmly believed that judges were lawyers just as we were. He would say that trials are a contest and lawyers are the players while the judge is simply the referee. I had taken to heart Harry's question, "What's with this Your Honor stuff? Call them what they are—Judges."

It was clear to me now that that attitude wasn't going to fly in federal court. At least this federal court.

This was one of my early federal court cases. I had cut my teeth in the Michigan state courts of general jurisdiction, known as circuit courts, where judges were basically elected politicians, and their courtroom behavior was often driven by a desire to be re-elected. Practically all my state court cases were jury trials, where the juries were all from the county in which the court sat. In Detroit, that was Wayne County.

Federal court was proving to be a bit more formal. Federal judges are appointed by the President of the United States pursuant to Article III of the United States Constitution and confirmed by the U.S. Senate. These judges are appointed for life. Once appointed, they owe no political favors. It is believed that our founding fathers intended this method to keep them free to objectively apply the law. Practically speaking, what it meant was that I had to play to the judge and would have to adjust accordingly.

Today we were in the federal court sitting in Flint, Michigan. The case was a wrongful death suit involving a Learjet model 23, the design of which was factually a contributing cause of the crash. We were here in Flint starting a trial against the United States. Yes, in some types of torts, the U.S. allows itself to be sued. However, cases against the U.S. have no juries. These cases are called federal tort claims cases.

In the Treu case, I was claiming that the air traffic controllers (a branch of the Federal Aviation Administration) were negligent and were a contributing cause of the crash.

On January 7, 1977, Donald Treu, a Learjet captain, had been flying in instrument conditions in the clouds, his plane being vectored by air traffic control (ATC) for an instrument approach to land on runway 18 at the Flint Bishop International Airport, serving Flint, Michigan. That was, he was being given compass headings to intercept the runway centerline. This particular instrument approach was referred to as an ILS-18. This would provide electronic guidance, displayed on the airplane's instruments, both directional guidance down the runway centerline and vertical guidance on a slope down to a landing spot. At this point in time, the ILS approach was the most regularly used precision approach when there was a low ceiling and/or low visibility.

The *Air Traffic Controller's Handbook* requires that the final vector to the runway centerline must be no more than a specified limited intercept angle. The final vector is required to be a small intercept angle to avoid steep turns. When the Learjet was cleared for the approach to runway 18, because of the intercept angle given by ATC was so great, the Learjet had to make a very steep turn and suffered an aerodynamic stall too close to the ground to recover. It fell out of the sky and crashed.

The Learjet model 23 was prone to this dangerous instability and uncontrollable behavior, but it was the ATC that had given a vector, which was an angle too big to allow a safe turn on to the final approach course. The resultant steep turn revealed Lear's poor design and dangerous stall characteristics.

All airplane wings will suffer an aerodynamic stall if the angle of attack is high enough. However, the pilot of a transportation airplane wants the stall characteristics to be as friendly and docile as practical. That is, pilots would like sufficient warning of the pending stall and a smooth loss of lift as compared to a sudden snap. The ability to quickly recover with a minimum loss of altitude is also important in an air transport.

Although many jets don't have great stall characteristics, the Learjet was below acceptable. When I first looked at the Learjet wing with its thin airfoil having a sharp leading edge and wingtip fuel tanks, I thought it might be a handful in a stall. The local hangar talk immediately after the plane appeared on the market backed up this hunch. Also, the Learjet was equipped with a stick shaker and stick pusher. The shaker warns the pilot that the airplane is near the stall angle of attack, while the pusher pushes the nose of the plane down to prevent a stall or to recover from the pending stall.

Many jets have stick shakers to give a stall warning, only a few designs with questionable stall characteristics come equipped with a pusher. At this point in time, very few designs required stick pushers. This in itself was a sign of the plane's instability.

The Treu case urged me to go beyond my own assumptions about the Learjet's bad aerodynamics characteristics and take a deep look into the plane's real capabilities. As was my usual tactic by now with these cases, I wanted to personally know how the plane performed in a stall. If nothing else, this would give me some extra tools when cross-examining Learjet employees and expert witnesses.

After a little research, which included NTSB and FAA files, conversations with Learjet test pilots, and a basic analysis of the geometry and mass distribution of the Learjet, I was ready to go flying. It wasn't so hard to find a Learjet to test. I simply found a nearby Learjet model 24, located the owner, and asked if I might lease the airplane for a couple of days. After some convincing, he agreed, but on the condition that his chief pilot would go along and fly the left seat.

I agreed to the terms, and the following day, his pilot and I climbed on board. We purposely had no passengers.

I sat in the right seat and did the radio work with air traffic control. When we had leveled off at twenty thousand feet above sea level, I asked the owner's pilot to do a couple of stalls. He agreed and began to slow the aircraft. He continued to slow and increase pitch until the stick shaker fired. He then added power and lowered the nose. He called this a stall recovery. When he'd leveled off, he said, "See, that's not so bad."

What he had done was the way that stalls were practiced in training, but it wasn't what I wanted to see, so I asked if I could perform a stall from the right seat. He said, "Sure."

I then called the controller and requested a block altitude from twenty to ten thousand feet. The pilot in the left seat asked why.

"Just being careful."

"Whatever," he said.

With these words, I then began a right turn, powered back, and pitched up. When the stall stick shaker began, I kept pulling right back into my lap. Immediately, the airplane pitched down sharply and rolled about ninety degrees to the right. Within seconds, the plane was nose down and entering a spin. It took about half of the ten thousand feet that the ATC had cleared for me to recover from the stall, and that was accomplished by applying the best possible technique, which I had prepared for. Additionally, I knew it was going to stall when it started, so I was ready. It could easily have taken many more thousand feet to recover if I hadn't known what was going to happen beforehand. I was sure Donald Treu had no idea he was going to stall or how long it would take to recover. Certainly, he would have hit the ground long before he had a chance.

Treu had other troubles as well. The air traffic controllers told him that he was three miles out from the final approach fix, when in fact he was eight. They also gave him too large of an intercept angle, which required an excessively sharp turn to get on the approach course and brought about the aerodynamic stall. These negligent acts contributed to the crash. However, in my mind, the defective design of the airplane was also a substantial cause of the crash. In this case, the design defect was the aerodynamic stall characteristics of the Learjet.

Another interesting note on the Treu case was that, oddly enough, Michael Moore, later of *Fahrenheit 911* and *Roger and Me* fame, was in the courtroom and taking notes during the trial. I was under the impression he was going to write an article. It would have been great if facts of the case were revealed to the public.

After the proofs were in, the judge in the Treu case found the air traffic controllers negligent and awarded fair damages. However, in my mind, this was bigger than just another case. There had been too many fatal Learjet crashes to simply be chalked up to pilot negligence, controller negligence, or bad weather. If ever there was a clear pattern of a poorly-designed plane and one very ill fitted for its actual use, then the Learjet was it.

The First Private Jet

By 1964, when the first Learjet hit the market, I was already out of Boeing and working for Continental Aviation while also attending law school. I didn't have time for much else besides work and study, so what flying I could do was out of Detroit City Airport. Additionally, I was on a Continental engineering team to develop a three-hundred-shaft-horsepower turbine engine for the U.S. Army's light observation helicopter. We were using a Bell 47 helicopter as a test bed and did most of our test flying at Detroit City Airport. What this meant was that I was still an airport bum and privy to much hangar talk and had a feel for what pilots and mechanics thought of the new Learjet. The gist of the hangar noise was, it should only be piloted by fearless "top guns" and was a tricky little bird.

The release of the first private jet was a big deal. At the time, there had been a couple of entrepreneurs trying to develop smaller corporate jets that could be bought for less than a million dollars. In 1964, there was a race to certification and, thus, market share between the Learjet and the Jet Commander. It was Lear who had famously won, subsequently making his name synonymous with private jets for decades. The likes of F. Lee Bailey, Frank Sinatra, and others of the rich and famous crowd were heard to say, "Pull out the Lear. We're going to Palm Springs, Miami or up to the city." However, there was a problem with the aircraft at the time, and still the concept is not fully understood. It was a problem that existed at the plane's inception, which had killed many more people than my client Donald Treu.

Bill Lear, whom I had briefly met, was a bright and eccentric inventor who had cut his teeth designing car radios. He had invented the eight-track tape system and even airplane autopilots.

After his string of successes, this turbulent man decided that he was going to get into the small corporate jet airplane business. Rather than start a new design on a fresh sheet of paper, a job clearly out of his league, he purchased the rights to a Swiss fighter trainer jet. This trainer had never really been in production. Two of its prototypes had crashed in Switzerland during flight testing.

Bill Lear decided to take this unsuccessful prototype of a fighter trainer and convert it into a hot-rod corporate jet transport.

Type Certificates and Design Standards

"Our Father who art in Washington, Halaby his name."

When I was at Boeing in flight test, the administrator of the Federal Aviation Administration was Najeeb Halaby. To us, he was like God. In our minds, it was he whom we had to please. "Our Father who art in Washington, Halaby his name."

In my time at Boeing, the primary task of the flight test department was to get the new models of the Boeing transport aircraft certified by the FAA. This piece of the development of a new design was time-consuming and terribly expensive. The task required extensive analysis, technical reports, and flight tests to demonstrate compliance with the standards of the Federal Air Regulations, known as FARs.

If successful, the model was granted a "type certificate." However, because of the cost and difficulty, when models grew in performance, passenger carrying capability, or to chase the state of the art, manufacturers negotiate to have the advanced models added to the existing type certificate rather than trying to earn a new type certificate.

Lear had big problems earning the type certificate for the first model, namely the Model 23. Certification of smaller airplanes that were under 12,500 lbs. maximum allowable gross weight were certified in accordance with a less strict set of standards as compared to larger air transports, specifically Part 23 of the FARs. Weight-wise, the Learjet fell under this less stringent set of rules. However, Part 23 didn't cover jets or airplanes requiring a crew of more than one pilot. All larger airplanes and those requiring a crew of two pilots or two pilots and a flight engineer or navigator were required to be certified under the more stringent standards of FAR Part 25.

Bill Lear started the certification process, intending to gain a type certificate for the Learjet model 23 under Part 23 of the FARs. He wanted to keep the selling price under a million dollars and the gross weight under 12,000 pounds, but trying to squeeze a high-performance jet into this category, which was really meant for little airplanes, was a nightmare. There were other problems as well: jet engines require high altitudes for efficiency, and along with the high altitudes comes pressurization issues. Along with pressurization issues come new structural issues and environmental issues. Time and cost start to grow and the problems go on. Bill Lear was starting to freak. In his mind, it was imperative to beat his competition to certification.

In the final analysis, the FAA stood fast and took the position that the aircraft must meet the stricter requirements of Part 25 of the FARs. Aside from this hiccup, the plane went through certification in record time. Presumably helped along by Lear's connections in Washington and by the fact that an FAA pilot crashed one of Lear's test planes.

The crash happened on a day in early June. An FAA test pilot was in the left seat as pilot-in-command, with a Lear test pilot acting as second-in-command. This was the Learjet prototype and Lear's only finished airplane at that time. The crew was conducting certification flight testing out of Mid-Continent Airport, Wichita, Kansas. At the time, they were in the process of evaluating takeoffs with one engine inoperative. On their last single-engine takeoff, which was a missed approach and go-around, the pilot failed to retract the speed brakes. As a result, the FAA pilot could not maintain the climb due to drag and loss of lift and was forced to put the bird down in a cornfield off the end of the runway. He did a pretty good job of performing this off-airport landing in the corn; however, a fuel tank was punctured, and the airplane caught fire and was destroyed.

The Lear staff were devastated. They realized that they were out of time and money, and worse yet, their only prototype had been destroyed.

Bill Lear saw things in a different light. After learning that no one was injured, he said, "Cheer up. We just sold our first airplane, and the U.S. government is the customer. They can afford it."

He also knew that his team had just then finished Learjet number 2, which had been fully paid for by his friend. He was sure that his friend would allow him to instrument number 2 and use it to finish certification testing. And with the FAA being terribly embarrassed, he had some leverage to accelerate the certification process. Bill Lear also threatened representatives of the FAA, telling them that he was going to call President Johnson, who would kick their asses all over Washington.

At least to some extent it worked.

Najeeb Halaby handed the type certificate to Lear on July 31, 1964, months before the Jet Commander, his competition, was certified. In my opinion, an opinion I later formed, the certification had been finalized well before the plane was ready.

Certified Poor Design

Such an opinion is borne out by the plane's subsequent history. About half of the Model 23 Learjet airplanes crashed; a majority were fatal. There were enough obvious problems that in the mid-1970s, the FAA decided it was necessary to review the original type certificate. This procedure was known as a Special Certification Review (SCR). During the SCR, the agency did extensive reviews, including analysis and flight testing. As a result, several modifications dealing with stability and control issues and crew warning issues were mandated.

Yet the Learjet quickly became very popular and remained popular notwithstanding continued safety problems. In fact, the height of their popularity coincides with the height of their accidents.

The safety problems were manyfold: the basic airplane geometry had been a poor choice for a transportation airplane, it was also the case that the FAA's design standards hadn't been written to cover small general aviation jets, and many of the systems, materials, instrument panels, emergency devices, and handling characteristics were substandard compared to the larger jet transports of the day and to what they should have been.

Making a Transport out of a Fighter Trainer

To start with, the design philosophy guiding transportation aircraft and military fighter airplanes is clearly different. Good engineering dictates that a transport be a stable platform with the tendency to return to the position chosen by the pilot or the autopilot when upset. For example, the plane should tend to return to straight and level flight and on course. On the other hand, the designers of a military combat or attack airplanes typically want the pilot to be able to maneuver quickly in roll, pitch, and yaw and don't want the craft to tend to return to its pre-selected position. Furthermore, the design architecture and weight distribution would be quite different between them and would include things like the selection of the airfoils (the cross-sectional shape of the wing and control surfaces). Additionally, the designer of a fighter airplane might want a wing with a symmetrical airfoil (same curve or chamber on the top as the bottom) so it could fly as well upside down as right side up. But of course, you don't want or need transportation airplanes flying upside down.

The Swiss fighter trainer also had wingtip fuel tanks, which aggravated the chance of an inadvertent entry into a spin when the airplane would experience an unintended aerodynamic stall, again an undesirable characteristic for a transport.

Simply put, Bill Lear started his dream airplane with the wrong type of airframe. Additionally, rushing to certify the aircraft in record time coupled with cost issues left the Learjet with numerous operational and safety problems. Several of these problems will be reflected in various product liability lawsuits as we move forward, most notably in *Taylor v. Learjet* and in the bird strike case both described below.

It was obvious from early on that the Learjet had troubles. Among the jet pilots and want-to-be jet pilots, all with rather large egos, the talk was that it took a "real pilot," or as the hangar talk went, "a real stick," to fly a Lear. Again, with the piston twins in the previous chapter a kind of bravado set in which saw flying unnecessary dangerous aircraft as a badge of honor, a sentiment that helped mute real investigation into the plane's poor qualities. It was clear to me that the airplane wasn't just fast and hard to fly; it was also unnecessarily dangerous.

After certification in the summer of 1964, the very high accident rate drove the Learjet Company and several other entrepreneurs to design and apply a cadre of band-aid upgrades and modifications to the Lear. Some helped more than others, and some had no effect at all, while others made things worse. This meant that of the Learjets in the sky at any given time in those early years, very few were original due to upgrades and retrofits. I heard some pilots and owners brag that they had "one of the good ones" as they put it, referring to the retrofits. All this meant was that people were aware of the plane's aerodynamic troubles, and while they still wanted to fly and to own one, they also knew they needed to fix them. One of these "fixes" would lead our firm to acquire a patent infringement case described below.

Wings were modified with "boundary layer energizers (BLE)." These were little strips with a triangular cross-section that energized the boundary of air between those molecules touching the surface of the wing and the free airstream. The boundary layer is easier to comprehend by visualizing a ball bearing dropped into a glass of oil and envisioning the flow pattern around the ball as it falls through the oil. That flow pattern is the boundary layer. Lift efficiency is better if we have a smooth flow of air over the wing surface as compared to a turbulent flow, which is what such modifications aim to achieve.

Another modification was the use of vortex generators (little vertical fins) attached to various flight surfaces either to improve the boundary layer or to increase effectiveness of the various control surfaces. Various stabilizing fins such as dorsal and ventral fins were added to the rear of the fuselage. And it goes on! Eventually, the wingtip fuel tanks were removed on later models.

Patent Infringement

The use of the BLEs also led to one of my noteworthy cases against Learjet, which further educated me on the granular details of the high-speed aerodynamic defects suffered by the Learjet. The device in question was invented by Dr. Arnold Kuethe, a professor of aerodynamics at the University of Michigan. He and Professor Chow authored a textbook that was used in one of my early courses in aerodynamics. Since Dr. Kuethe was an employee of the university, his patent inured to the university.

I received a call from a lawyer at the university asking if I would be interested in trying a patent infringement case on a contingent fee basis. This meant that I only got paid if I won. In such a case, it would be a percentage of the verdict. I was fine with the arrangement. In fact, I preferred it. But there was one small problem.

"I don't know anything about patents," I told him.

"That's okay. We do, and we'll teach you what you need to know. You are an engineer and a good trial lawyer. That's what we need," he responded.

I had learned a lot about the Learjet by this time and thought I could learn a lot more, so I took the case. The case would certainly allow me to learn more about aerodynamics, which I always enjoyed. It further gave me entry to a new area of law, and with the university's expertise on my side, this seemed exciting.

After looking at the possible jurisdictions and venues, I filed the case in federal court in Phoenix, Arizona.

On the day of trial, when the case was called and the judge asked us to stand and state our appearances, I rose and stated, "Richard Schaden for the plaintiff, the University of Michigan."

Judge McNamee responded dryly, "That's a pretty fancy client you have."

I wondered where he was going with this.

"I want to tell you," he continued, "this is a PAC-8 court not a BIG-10 court."

Now I saw what he was getting at. He continued, "One of your opponents was my professor in law school, and I really liked him. Do you still want to try your case in this court?"

I grinned. "Judge," I responded, "I don't know a lot about patents, and I am not sure if the court does [having done my homework]. But all those guys in silk suits over at the defense table, they know a lot about patents. I think you and I are going to learn a lot in the next few months."

"Few months?" he said, surprised.

"That's about what I think it will take. Let's have fun."

In fact, the case would take two months.

PhDs in aeronautics and fluid flow experts from several fancy universities testified, including a few from Germany. I remember at least once a young assistant professor from one of the noteworthy schools gave an opinion on something related to boundary layer energy, and Dr. Kuethe, who was in his late nineties at the time and sitting with me at counsel table, jumped up, shaking his finger, "Sonny, you are wrong."

The judge politely said, "Please, Doctor, will you sit down."

In preparation for cross-examination, I had read every book on aerodynamics and fluid mechanics that I could get my hands on. I memorized the applicable equations. It was what I called bathtub knowledge. I would learn so much for cross-examination, and then after the trial, it was like I'd pulled the plug, and so much of that knowledge went down the drain.

The defense case was substantively weak. The jury gave a verdict of willful infringement, which allowed for more than ordinary damages. They awarded a substantial sum to the University of Michigan. Shortly thereafter, Learjet was sold to Bombardier. It seems that the differences between the PAC-8 and BIG-10 and Judge McNamee's affection for his old law school professor didn't get in the way of justice. For some time thereafter, when I was in Phoenix, I would stop and have coffee with the judge.

Taylor v. Learjet

About the same time as the Treu case, we brought *Taylor v. Learjet*, which was probably one of the largest verdicts of any of our Learjet cases. It further highlighted some of the plane's basic design defects.

My client, Jimmy Taylor, was a Learjet pilot. In September 1977, he was flying his boss, the chairman of Champion Homebuilding Co., the boss's wife, and one of the company employees back home to Flint, Michigan after a short business trip to Sanford, North Carolina. Jimmy, his co-pilot, the three passengers, and the boss's dog all died in the fiery crash shortly after takeoff. Witnesses saw the rear end of the airplane in flames as it climbed steeply through about three thousand feet. Next, they saw it go completely out of control and plunge in a ball of fire to the ground. It's highly probable that the fire in the rear compartment of the airplane had started before takeoff.

This was a wrongful death product liability case brought by his surviving wife against Learjet and the dealer who sold the airplane to his boss. The fire started in the rear tail cone, affectionately known as the hell hole because it contains fuel valves, pumps, the ship's battery, and other electrical and mechanical equipment. It got that name because it is not a very friendly or comfortable place to work and/or inspect. This is a perfect place for a fire to start. The claim was that this tail cone compartment should have had a fire detector, which could advise the crew, and a fire extinguisher.

The venue was Wayne County Circuit Court located in Detroit, Michigan. The presiding judge was Arthur Bowman, a quite liberal and understanding judge. The jurors were from the heart of Detroit. I was by myself representing Mrs. Taylor. I was dressed in my signature Western pants, cowboy boots, and corduroy jacket. At the defense table, as usual, there were several insurance defense lawyers dressed in matching dark suits. Jimmy's wife had been pregnant at the time of the crash, but by trial, their daughter had grown into the cutest little two-year-old. I had her in the courtroom with us as much as possible. From time to time, I'd have her sit on my lap. In fact, at one point, I was holding her while I cross-examined one of Lear's expert witnesses.

The jury awarded Mrs. Taylor 2.5 million dollars in damages. Today the design regulations of the Federal Aviation Administration require fire detection and a fire extinguisher in these compartments, which can be seen and activated by the crew. Many of these types of cases resulted in life-saving changes in the design regulations and many other safety improvements.

Sunken Lunken and the Common Loon

So, let's call this next Learjet case the loon case. It's a tragic story worth telling.

Just after eleven o'clock on a Tuesday morning in April, the control tower at Cincinnati Municipal Airport heard Captain Woodworth transmit, "LUNKEN TOWER, LEAR FOUR ZERO PAPA GOLF READY FOR TAKEOFF RUNWAY 3 RIGHT." At this time, the captain had less than five minutes to live. The Lear was cleared for takeoff and to climb runway heading to five thousand feet. At thirty-eight hundred feet, the plane collided with a common loon, a bird weighing maybe three pounds. There were no passengers that day. Captain Woodworth was seated in the co-pilot's seat. He was instructing the younger, less-experienced pilot who sat in the captain's seat on the left side.

The loon crashed into the right-side windshield, entering the cockpit and decapitating Captain Woodworth. The bird and the pilot's head went through the cabin and smacked into the aft pressure bulkhead of the fuselage. At the same time, the hole in the windshield caused the cabin to depressurize, and debris rushed out through the breach. This debris was then sucked into the right engine, which caused it to flame out. The plane was now flying on only one engine, with half of the windshield missing. Air was howling through the hole in the windshield in excess of 150 miles per hour, and the hydraulic pump necessary to extend the landing gear and the wing flaps for landing was now inoperative.

Imagine this young, inexperienced pilot with a broken airplane, a headless man beside him, and a cockpit full of blood. He displayed a better-than-expected reaction and managed to turn the plane around, avoiding the many hills surrounding the area and returned to Sunken Lunken. (The airport was affectionately referred to as "Sunken Lunken" because it sat down in a valley that was often foggy with poor visibility.) This mist added to the young pilot's workload. He had cranked the landing gear down by hand and landed safely.

He survived the ordeal, but what about Captain Woodworth? Had the windshield survived the impact of the bird, Kent Woodworth would most likely have lived. Bird strikes had been a known hazard to flight forever. Bird encounters became a greater issue of concern with the advent of jets because of the speed and the possibility that they could be sucked into a jet engine inlet. The Learjet would have been required by the FAA during certification to convince the administrator that the windshield could withstand the impact of a four-pound bird at cruising speed. Note that the plane in question was climbing, thus quite a bit below cruising speed when it impacted the loon. Also of interest was that we had learned in the discovery phase of the lawsuit about the method Lear used to demonstrate compliance to the FAA. Basically, they had shot four-pound frozen chickens at the stationary windshield out of an air cannon. Interesting!

The question on my mind was, how big was the bird that struck the Lear? The NTSB report implied that it was an eight-pound bird. I questioned this assessment. I took that case believing that after reassessing the weight issue, the bird would get substantially smaller. Eight pounds seemed heavy for a loon; that's practically the weight of a Christmas turkey. But I hadn't yet decided how I would deal with this pivotal issue.

It was at this time that I began spending a good deal of time in Colorado, where I would eventually move.

One November day in Colorado, I had stopped at the *Loaf and Jug* convenience store just off the interstate highway I-70 in Golden, Colorado when a tall blond woman riding a Harley with a Saint Bernard in a sidecar pulled in next to me.

The whole image seemed curious. I approached her and commented on her dog, and we started to talk. As it turned out, she was good friends with one of my partners and had gone to law school with him. She then reminded me that we had met earlier at some function, which I didn't remember. Her name was Ann. In addition to being a law school graduate studying for the bar exam, she was an M.D., board-certified in pathology.

It was the week before Thanksgiving. She explained that her entire family lived on the East Coast near Baltimore where she really wanted to go for the holiday but couldn't due to tight finances. I was thinking about the bird strike case, and all of a sudden, I took our meeting as a stroke of good fortune.

The fact was that the NTSB had taken control of a wad of frozen biomatter from the aft pressure bulkhead of the subject Learjet.

The Board was storing this post-crash evidence in a freezer at the Smithsonian in Washington, D.C.

My wheels were turning. I ended up making a deal with her. I'd pay for her trip back east for Thanksgiving if she would work as a consultant and possible expert witness in the Woodworth case. She was a pathologist after all. My goal was to have her examine the wad of frozen material at the Smithsonian and determine its weight and the identity of the biomatter.

She liked the offer and left a couple of days later. I made arrangements with the defendant Learjet, the court, and the NTSB to have Dr. Ann McFarland examine the bio evidence. Late in the afternoon on the Friday after Thanksgiving, I received a call. Dr. Ann informed me that the majority of the matter that was weighed by the NTSB and believed to be loon was in fact my client's brain and skull plate. It turned out that the loon was substantially less than four pounds.

The reassessment of the bird's weight was accepted by the court and worked strongly in our favor. It also made a great impression on the jury. I further left the defendant in disarray when I called their in-house counsel as my first witness.

On the stand, he had no choice but to admit the weight of the loon. The fact that the Learjet windshield couldn't withstand the impact of a bird weighing less than four pounds at a speed below cruising speed was one of the first items of evidence that the jury heard. They heard this information directly from one of Learjet's officers and their lawyer just after I had told them in my opening statement what the evidence would show. Primacy is very significant in any presentation. In a jury trial, the opening statement, the first witness, and the first impressions of the lawyers and the plaintiff will be in the juror's heads throughout the trial. You don't want to spend the rest of the trial playing catch-up after a bad or a weak beginning.

We won the bird strike case. In part it was due to technique. But it was a sound case. The windshield of this airplane did not meet the minimum standards of the Federal Air Regulations. The integrity of the cockpit structure is of paramount importance. Since this case and other unfortunate occurrences, the analysis and testing of aircraft windshields have tightened up substantially.

There were several other Learjet cases tried and/or settled over the years. I wanted to believe that these lawsuits resulted in substantial safety-related changes in the Learjet and some changes in the Federal Air Regulations' minimum design standards.

CHAPTER 9

Northwest Airlines Flight 255

Neil Armstrong was the first man to walk on the moon when he put his foot down in the sea of Tranquility on the moon's surface, saying,
"That's one small step for man, and one giant leap for mankind."

It was August 16, 1987.

Northwest Airlines Flight 255 from Detroit to Phoenix began like any other, but when Captain John Maus and First Officer David Dobbs prepared for takeoff, they missed something. They hadn't configured the plane per their own calculations and failed to select the proper flap setting.

Such an oversight would almost certainly prove catastrophic, except the newly installed crew advisory system on the MD-80 and the model DC-9 should have warned the pilots of their oversight.

After all, that's what it was there for. This system was known as the Central Aural Warning System (CAWS) and typically sounded with a strange robotic voice. However, something had gone wrong there too, and on this warm summer night, the CAWS remained silent as the crew proceeded to takeoff.

It's normal for a flight crew to run a quick check before crossing the hold line onto the departure runway. We call it the FATS check: flaps, airbrakes, trims, and speeds. But somehow, they missed the fact that their flaps were in the wrong position.

There isn't just one single configuration that pilots must engage at takeoff. It really depends on the airplane, density altitude, runway length, etc. Given whatever the conditions are, the pilot may have some options especially at a major airport where runways are longer than needed. However, any final configuration needs to be consistent and checked against the V-speeds in jet transports. These speeds are critically important. In 1987, the speeds would have been calculated by tabular data in airplane operating manuals, which these days is all done by computers.

The speeds are as follows: V_1, V_r, and V_2.

V_1 is the point of no return, the (stop-go) speed. Before V_1, there is enough runway length to abort the flight. After V_1, you're "going flying" because there isn't enough runway to stop, that is, assuming the runway length is used in the V speed calculation.

V_r is rotation speed: the speed at which the flying pilot pulls back on the control and pitches the nose up. V_2 is the minimum speed the crew will climb with one engine inoperative. But the speeds aren't absolute, at least not from flight to flight, runway to runway, day to day, and season to season. They're based on things like flaps setting, airplane weight, wind, atmospheric pressure, temperature, runway altitude above mean sea level, runway length, and runway slope.

In the case of Flight 255, the crew had calculated the V speeds based on the flaps being in an extended position but took off with them fully retracted.

In addition, according to the cockpit voice recorder, the CAWS system didn't give them the aural warning, as it should have, when they advanced the power levers.

It's possible that both pilots had their attention diverted by nearby thunderstorms building to the north and northeast. Captain Maus was no rookie pilot. He had flown commercial airplanes for over thirty years and logged over twenty thousand hours of flight time. But this flight would be his last.

As the flying pilot attempted to rotate into the vee-bars (a little orange chevron on the primary flight display [PFD] instrument in front of the pilot), the plane never got more than fifty feet off the ground. It "flew" off the end of the runway. One wing hit a light pole. The plane went inverted, impacted the roof of an Avis Rental Car facility, and skidded upside down onto the adjacent street where it disintegrated and burst into flames.

First responders arrived in minutes and encountered a horrible crash site of twisted metal and dismembered and burning bodies. It appeared that no one could have lived. They stood there overwhelmed by the mayhem. Yet almost immediately, one of them heard a faint cry coming from the debris on the roadway. It turned out to be the lone survivor, a four-year-old girl still buckled into her seat face down in street.

Her name was Cecelia Cichan. She had suffered a fractured skull, severe burns, and a broken arm, but she was alive. Her mother, father, and six-year-old brother lay dead only a few feet away. Cecelia had likely survived because her mother had shielded her with her own body as the plane began to crash.

Several entire families had been killed that day. One small boy was flying alone for the first time. His parents only learned what happened when they arrived at the airport in Phoenix to pick him up.

Jim Tuck, a good friend of mine, also died. He was a trial lawyer specializing in product liability cases. He was on his way to take a deposition in the Phoenix area.

So far, my practice had been focused on general aviation crashes, but I had been becoming more and more aware of mass air disasters and was interested in getting involved, hoping that I could make a difference. Up to this time, I just hadn't been hired in cases involving any big jet airliners, where the lives of hundreds of passengers hung in the balance because of design and design-induced pilot error. I did represent passengers in an Alleghany Airlines twin turboprop Convair 580 that crashed on the final approach to Bradford, Pennsylvania, on Christmas Eve just after I got out of law school. However, the issues there were rather sophomoric.

Things were about to change. As airliners kept growing in passenger capacity and extended ranges over large bodies of open sea, mass disasters in the form of airplane crashes were like a recurring nightmare.

I was still at Boeing when I saw how marketing, economic issues, and even politics could have undue influence on airplane design. I first saw it when I was assigned to be a flight-test representative at a preliminary design meeting for the B737.

I got my first close look at a mass air disaster when that American Airlines B707 crashed in Jamaica Bay when I worked at Boeing. But there were other major crashes that had made spectacular news, like the collision of two B747s in the Canary Islands where nearly six hundred died.

What these crashes proved was that airline travel was not just a matter of life or death for individuals. Hundreds could die in the blink of an eye based on one oversight in engineering, piloting, air traffic control, maintenance, or a combination thereof. The case of a few people dying in the crash of a Learjet or a small general aviation airplane was tragic. But where hundreds were dying and large families were being snuffed out in seconds, it was intolerable.

The kind of mistakes that happened in Northwest Flight 255 had to be prevented in the future. There will always be some pilot error. Humans will make mistakes, but we needed to have crew advisory systems, warning systems, and prevention systems that really worked, or else, what were they for?

It was becoming my personal commitment to be a force to fix bad and inadequate airplane design issues.

Multidistrict Litigation

Lawyers representing all the passengers filed suits against both Northwest Airlines and McDonnell Douglas. The cases all ended up consolidated in multidistrict litigation (MDL), a special legal procedure designed to expedite the process of handling large, complex cases, which Northwest Flight 255 clearly was. A panel of federal district judges sit physically in the United States Supreme Court courtroom as the "multidistrict litigation panel." This panel assigns all the cases filed in a mass disaster to a designated federal district court. The Flight 255 cases were sent to Chief Judge Julian Cook in Detroit, Michigan.

However, I had a reputation for preferring state courts, and so before the case was sent to Detroit, I appeared before the multidistrict litigation panel at the United States Supreme Court. As I approached the podium, Federal Judge Brenner of Colorado joked, "And here comes Mr. Schaden with his never-ending quest to stay out of federal court." Judge Brenner and I weren't strangers. He was a federal judge in Denver.

At the time, there had been talk about forcing all airline disaster cases into the federal system, which had never been mandatory before.

When the case got to Detroit, Judge Cook appointed me and four other passengers' lawyers to the plaintiff's steering committee. This was a good thing for attorneys specializing in airline disaster cases. The steering committee is in charge of discovery and often in trying the case. In those days, lawyers were not permitted to advertise. Being on the committee was an effective marketing strategy. It produced substantial media coverage, helping acquire future business.

By the mid-1980s, I would be appointed to the steering committee in most of the major airline disaster cases in United States federal courts. I had an edge over most lawyers requesting these appointments because I had a technical understanding of the aircraft, courtroom experience, and air-transport pilot experience, which was somewhat unique at the time.

Chief Judge Cook divided the passengers' case against Northwest Airlines and McDonnell Douglas into two phases. First, we would try the case on liability to determine who was at fault. The plan was that the damages suffered by the passengers and those killed on the ground would later be determined at a subsequent trial.

In their defense, Northwest claimed that the CAWS system should have warned the pilots that the airplane was not properly configured for takeoff. A strong case could be made on the warning issue. We all knew from the cockpit voice recorder (CVR), the device that records all the sounds in the cockpit including the radio transmissions, that there had not been any aural warning. In addition to voice, this "black box" used a cockpit area microphone that records the noises made by the airplane systems and equipment. Such sounds might include clicks, pumps, air noises, metal grinding, etc. We used a system known as sound spectrum analysis to identify what the various noises meant.

The question came down to the fact that had the crew been warned by the CAWS system, they would have aborted before V_1 was reached, and likely the crash never would have happened. While acknowledging pilot error, Northwest cross-claimed against McDonnell Douglas, arguing that the failed warning system was a contributing cause of the crash, which it clearly was. In their defense, McDonnell Douglas denied liability and claimed that the Northwest crew had intentionally pulled the circuit breaker for the CAWS system because they thought it was irritating to have the warning constantly going off for one reason or another. Pulling circuit breakers on irritating systems wasn't outside the realm of possibility as it had been known to happen. This was a time when synthesized voice systems were just starting to be used and sounded a bit strange and annoying.

This aspect of the case revolved around why the CAWS did not alert the crew: was the critic breaker pulled, or was it a malfunction?

McDonnell Douglas had no direct evidence that the circuit breaker had been pulled. There was nothing on the CVR to support it. What this meant was that the defendant needed to use circumstantial evidence to make the jury believe that it happened. Even though this seems like a minor issue, this is the ground on which the battle would be fought.

I also couldn't help but think, *Did the lives of over a 150 people really hang on the condition of a single circuit breaker?* Of course, I knew small issues like this could bring planes down, but to see 150 people dead over such a malfunction, if that was what it was, was sobering to say the least, which made the argument over why the CAWS failed all the more important since in order to make the system safer in the future, we had to know what happened.

Northwest argued that the circuit breaker was bad and should not have been used nor located as it was in the CAWS warning system. Further, there was some evidence pointing to irregularities on the contact surfaces of the breaker, and we used a scanning electron microscope to make the argument. Making matters more confusing, we heard conflicting expert opinions on the conclusions that were drawn by the magnified pictures of the contact surfaces of the circuit breaker. The experts had pictures of these contact surfaces blown up three thousand times using scanning electron microscopes.

Another issue worth noting was the fact that the MD-80 was certified by the FAA on the same type certificate as the DC-9, which was a significantly smaller airplane. The DC-9 carried about half as many passengers as the MD-80 that crashed in Detroit, had much smaller engines, and a lower maximum allowable takeoff weight, about half as much as the MD-80.

The FAA had not required McDonnell Douglas to earn a new certificate. Somehow, the FAA had been convinced that the MD-80 was similar enough to the original DC-9 that it didn't require a completely new certificate and certification program—was this a technical decision or a political one? As I got further into the case, I began to wonder how this could be. Were the lobbyists and the political influence this powerful?

It was at this point that I began to clearly see the phantom forces lurking around these airline disaster cases.

Charles "Pete" Conrad

While the case itself was argued over minor issues and over the division of blame, which was relatively procedural and insignificant compared to arguing the flight characteristics of a Learjet, of particular interest was the first name on the list of witnesses. Pete Conrad was the first name I noticed. He had been an astronaut and as crew on the Apollo 12 trip and was the third man to walk on the moon. Furthermore, he had been a Navy test pilot and an aeronautical engineer. As résumés for expert witnesses go, he was among the best.

At the time of trial, my research showed him to be a vice president of McDonnell Douglas, along with many other notable accomplishments. Despite all he had done in and around aeronautics, I wasn't sure what his purpose was as an expert. Neither his career nor his experience told me that he designed or piloted airline transports. While it was a big accomplishment, "what did walking on the moon" have to do with the crash of an MD-80 or a failed CAWS system? He was a corporate officer working in the marketing department at McDonnell Douglas. My assumption was that they simply wanted him to wrap the MD-80 in the American flag and send it to the moon. It was his credibility they counted on, not his particular expertise.

Pertaining to his credibility, however, I ran across a picture of Conrad in the *New York Times*, where he was dressed in a space suit with the actor Jimmy Stewart in a flight suit, beside actress and model Bo Derek in hot pants. The caption under the picture said, "Astronaut Pete Conrad teams up with Jimmy Stewart and Bo Derek to enhance the failing image of the McDonnell Douglas Airplane Company."

American hero or not, it seemed that enhancing McDonnell's failing image was Conrad's function here as well. I stuck this photo in my case and marked it as an "exhibit for identification." I didn't tell anyone about it. No one, including the steering committee, knew about the picture. But I had a plan for getting it into evidence.

While there was considerable debate among the plaintiff's steering committee as to who exactly would cross-examine Conrad, somehow, I prevailed. While I was looking forward to this cross-examination, I knew I had to be very careful and show respect for such an American hero. There was a fine line between attacking the credibility of his company and showing disrespect for an astronaut who was a hero in the minds of Americans. If I crossed that line, I would lose a lot of ground.

Now there was practically nothing to this case. Pretty much everything had been admitted by the parties. That is, Northwest was operating the airplane what the law refers to as a "common carrier." Common carriers are liable if they are for negligent for the death or injuries suffered by its passengers. Common carriers are held to a very high standard. Northwest admitted that they took off with the airplane improperly configured, so they were negligent.

The United States, in general, follows common law, which is a body of law derived from English law. For the most part, "common law" is based on precedent and custom rather than written statutes or code. In common law, there is a doctrine known as *res ipsa loquitur*, which in Latin means "the thing speaks for itself." In the crash of Flight 255, the facts pretty much spoke for themselves. So, the long and protracted trial was a fight between Northwest and McDonnell Douglas over a circuit breaker, and since there was a fair dispute among experts over why the CAWS system failed, this argument was going to come down to credibility, and from my view, Pete

Conrad's credibility would go to the credibility of McDonnell Douglas's defense.

After he sang the praises of the MD-80, it was my turn to cross-examine.

I don't often script what I'm going to say in court. I do generally have a list of single words to jog my memory if needed, but going on feelings usually works the best for me. In this case, since I knew I had to be careful how I handled him, I wanted to make astronaut Conrad feel good, praise him for his accomplishments, while at the same time showing the jury why he had really been called as an expert. His appearance was an obvious stunt by McDonnell Douglas, and that was what I wanted the jury to see clearly.

I stood and thanked Mr. Conrad for taking time out of his busy and important schedule and for traveling all the way from California to share his courageous endeavors with us here in Detroit. I then said, "Mr. Conrad, I've never walked on the moon, and I don't think that any of the ladies or gentlemen of the jury have ever walked on the moon, but the judge thinks he's walked on the moon."

Glancing at the jury, I saw a few chuckles. Before I got the rest of the question out, though, the judge, *sua sponte* (without a formal prompting), started hammering with his gavel.

I immediately said, "I'll withdraw the question."

The judge replied, "Mr. Schaden, move on."

Next, I said, "How did you get to know Bo Derek?"

The defense jumped up, "Objection, irrelevant."

Now the judge was pissed. "I'm going to put an end to this! Counsel, approach the bench."

I grabbed the picture from the *New York Times* that I had in my possession and went up to the bench as I had been told to do. I tossed the proposed marked exhibit up in front of the judge, but he didn't look at it.

"Enough shenanigans, Schaden," he replied.

I responded, "I'm sorry, Your Honor. I'll move on," and returned to the lectern, leaving the article with the picture and caption "Astronaut Pete Conrad teams up with Jimmy Stewart and Bo Derek to enhance the failing image of the McDonnell Douglas Airplane Company," on the bench for Judge Cook. This time, I started with something that sounded like a totally different question. "Mr. Conrad, you're a famous astronaut, walked on the moon, an excellent test pilot, and an aeronautical engineer. You could have joined any company you wanted. Why did you join a company that had such a failing image?" Again, the judge *sua sponte* objected. But the witness put up his hand and said, "Judge, I would like to answer that question."

With that, I saw Judge Cook glance down at the proposed exhibit that I had tossed onto the bench. "Okay, Mr. Conrad, go ahead," he said.

The witness continued, "I picked McDonnell Douglas because it had such a sterling image."

With that, the picture went into evidence and was shown to the jury. Conrad had just opened the door to allowing an exhibit that normally would have been hearsay. I could now refer to the picture throughout the trial and use it in closing arguments. It went a long way to proving my point that McDonnell Douglas was using the famous astronaut to rehab its own less-than-stellar image. On the issue of the credibility and McDonnell Douglas having called this American hero as a witness, I also wanted to show that while Conrad was famous and an expert in his way, he wasn't all that familiar with airline transport procedures, which would further show that he was there to clean up the company's image.

A technique in examining expert witnesses is the use of hypothetical questions, and I wanted to set up a hypothetical cockpit in the courtroom and ask some questions about takeoff procedures. I thought it would illustrate my point better than by using a series of questions.

I asked the court if we could put a couple of chairs in front of the jury box to simulate the pilot and co-pilot in an MD-80. Somewhat surprising to me, Judge Cook seemed to like the idea. I asked the witness to sit in the left chair and to play the hypothetical captain as I sat in the right chair as his co-pilot, asking the questions.

After arranging the courtroom to fit my needs and we were seated in our "pilot" and "co-pilot" seats, I began by saying, "Now, Captain Conrad, assume that ATC at the Detroit Metro tower cleared Northwest Flight 255 to taxi into position and hold on runway 3 center. Assume further that your radar showed thunderstorms covering about 60 percent of the sky about 5 to 10 miles off the end of the runway and that we have 150 passengers onboard. Assume further that ATIS has reported a crosswind of 15 to 25 gusts. Also assume that we have determined the V speeds based on a given flap position, atmospheric pressure, ambient temperature, the reported wind, and the airplane's weight as loaded. Assume that you have told your first officer that you want standard calls. You are then cleared for takeoff to maintain runway heading to 3,000 feet. Now you can advance the power levers to takeoff power."

I then called out, "Acceleration good, airspeed alive both sides, 80 knots abort, number one engine," but Conrad didn't respond. His hand was still forward, indicating power levers still in the takeoff position. We continue to accelerate. We pass through V_1 on the airspeed indicator. I say, "We've just crashed. We can try again, but pilots of airline transports don't get a do-over."

We stayed in the chairs as I continued my cross-examination and went through a number of procedures that were pretty basic for airline operations. I kept it rather lighthearted. He was obviously very talented and a very nice man. As to this operation, he answered some things right and others wrong. The jury and Judge Cook seemed to enjoy our little tête-à-tête. But it was clear that he was in the marketing department and his job at McDonnell Douglas was to enhance its failing image and not to be a line pilot on an MD-80. I had made the point delicately enough not to damage my own standing in the eye of the jury, but also not too roughly take down an obviously well-liked American hero. We even had some fun while doing it.

After many months in trial, all parties reached a settlement. The best part was the aftermath. The aircraft industry, along with the electronic companies, really went to work on flight crew warning and advisory systems. Today, every jet transport uses very effective crew advisory systems that are both audio and visual. Nowadays, the systems are referred to as CAS (crew advisory systems). This case and other cases wherein experts exchanged ideas as to the cause of crashes and discussed remedial measures were a great impetus for the use of crew advisory and warning systems. It was a level intercourse above what went on in company engineering departments

The trial of the Northwest Airlines Flight 255 disaster was long, approximately thirteen months. The court and jury listened to many expert witnesses, saw demonstrative evidence, and evaluated the issue of cockpit annunciators and warning systems. A large settlement in this negligence and product liability case was a relatively cheap price paid to have likely saved many lives thereafter.

CHAPTER 10

United Airlines Flight 811

When I have fears that I may cease to be.

—*John Keats*

It was February 1989. A faceless airline booking computer had assigned the man from New Zealand the business class seat 8H. He died along with eight other passengers after being blown out of a large hole in the side of Boeing 747-122 aircraft during an explosive decompression at twenty-three thousand feet above the Pacific Ocean. The same computer had assigned seat 7B in business class to a Denver aviation attorney, my partner, Bruce Lampert. He lived. He was on the upper deck of the mammoth jumbo jet.

Bruce had joined our small boutique law firm shortly after we opened our Denver office. He has an identical twin brother, Brian, who is also a lawyer. Sometimes they would substitute and appear in court for each other. For the most part, the judges didn't know the difference.

Bruce had been working around the clock, taking depositions in the Northwest Airlines 255 case (Chapter 9). He had been traveling to California every Monday and coming back to Denver each Friday night. He lived this way for weeks. As a perk of those weeks of air travel to McDonnell Douglas in Long Beach, Bruce had accumulated thousands of mileage points. He had decided to use those points and set out on a bucket list journey to New Zealand and Australia. It was this trip that put him on United Airlines Flight 811.

United Airlines Flight 811 took off from Honolulu, Hawaii, in the early morning hours of February 24, 1989. Onboard were the flight crew, 15 flight attendants, and 337 passengers. The pilot-in-command was Captain David Cronin, fifty-nine, and only one flight from the FAA-mandated retirement at age sixty. He had a total of 28,000 hours of flight time, 1,700 in the Boeing 747. Important to later events, Captain Cronin was an experienced glider pilot with hundreds of hours in powerless aircraft. Seated next to Captain Cronin was First Officer Gregory Slader, age forty-eight, and sitting sideways behind Greg was the Flight Engineer Randall Thomas age forty-six.

Flight 811 departed Honolulu gate 10 at 01:33 Honolulu time. The flight engineer reported that all cabin and cargo door warning lights were out prior to the plane's departure from the gate. The captain was at the controls when the flight was cleared for takeoff on runway 8 right at 1:52 local time.

This was said by Bruce:

"We weren't the friskiest group of passengers ever seen on an airplane. Many of us were on the airplane since it left Los Angeles seven hours earlier. Most of us were looking for a pillow, a blanket and asking the cabin crew to turn off the lights. I think it was the intention of most of the passengers to turn over and go to sleep. As it rolled down the runway for takeoff, it was approximately 6 o'clock in the morning back in Denver where I had departed. I had a Walkman with earphones listening to former Kingston Trio singer and

now California activist and painter, John Stewart, singing his 1989 single, "Strange Rivers." I had taken off my shoes and put on the slippers provided for business class overseas flights."

The flight crew reported the plane's operation to be normal during takeoff and initial climb. The flight crew observed en route thunderstorms both visually and on the airplane's weather radar and requested a deviation from air traffic control. Because of the thunderstorms, Captain Cronin elected to leave the seat belt sign "on." This was just one of the numerous decisions made by the flight crew that night that saved lives.

"We were reclining and relaxing during the climb out. The cabin crew were not disturbing passengers in that the seat belt sign was still illuminated. Suddenly, there was a bang, a sudden roar, as the pressurized air escaped the aircraft. Everything that was not fastened down became airborne. The plastic panels that had covered the green aluminum structure blew out from their attachments and became airborne. The chandelier that had previously hung over the stairwell to the deck below was ripped out of the ceiling and dangled by a cord.

"I looked to my right and there was a gap the size of a basketball in the skin of the starboard side of the aircraft. One of the upper deck windows had been breached and bent tortuously out of its frame. I saw stark terror on the whitened faces of my fellow passengers. To my right were a middle-aged couple from Boulder, Colorado and another couple from Seattle. They were panicked. The husbands grabbed their wives and pulled them toward them, toward the inside of the airplane, away from the twisted window frame. One was holding his wife so hard that his knuckles were white. It was a hold. It was an embrace that said, 'I am going to die with the person I love.'

"I was seated next to a man I did not know. I didn't want to hug him and I certainly did not want to die with him. I was alone. I realized that I was going to die alone. My heroic quest was going to end in tragedy. My mind did quick a comparison with the sequence of TWA 800, a mass disaster crash with which I was quite familiar. TWA 800—747, climb out, explosion, decompression, and partial breakup...I could not complete the sequence in my mind...the logical step was too horrible to even formalize in my mind. So, I went back to the beginning, 747 climb out, explosion, decompression, partial breakup. STOP, Can't go on. Can't be true. Not happening. This is a movie, a bad dream. A person's mind is a complex and beautiful thing. If your mind receives input from your senses, eyes, ears, taste and body movement that is just too awful to contemplate, it shuts down. It doesn't process data. It goes into denial. This can't/isn't happening. If your brain tells you it is not happening and you go into denial, you have no reason to be afraid.

"I also strongly recommend adrenalin. It's a strong drug. Evolved from thousands of years of fight or flight. It is what you need in a crisis situation. It shocks you into action. Having been a survival officer in my Navy squadron as a collateral duty, I had given countless lectures to fighter crews on having a 'survival plan.' You need to know in advance what you're going to do in a crisis because you are not going to have time to think. But, the irony of being a passenger on a commercial airliner is that you are totally helpless. Here strapped into your seat in a completely full 747, nowhere to go, no one can hear you scream, nothing you can do. Your life is in the hands of three professionals on the other side of that cockpit door."

The flight crew stated that the first indication of a problem occurred while the airplane was climbing between twenty-two thousand and twenty-three thousand feet at an indicated airspeed (IAS) of three hundred knots. They heard a sound, described as a "thump," which shook the airplane. They said that this sound was followed immediately by a "tremendous explosion." The airplane had experienced an explosive decompression. They said that they donned their respective oxygen masks but found no oxygen available. The airplane cabin altitude horn sounded, and the flight crew believed the passenger oxygen masks had deployed automatically.

The captain immediately initiated an emergency descent and began dumping the fuel to lighten the aircraft for landing. The emergency checklist for in-flight decompression called for a lowering of the landing gear to expedite the descent. When Captain Cronin got to that step in the procedure, he thought, *no, not going to do that.* Varying from an emergency checklist is a significant decision for a pilot. This was the second of the captain's intuitive twenty-eight thousand flight hours command decisions. He held the landing gear. What was learned later was that the forward cargo door had suffered an un-commanded opening in-flight. Once the door was driven open electrically past a certain angle, it was caught in the airstream of a three hundred knot climb. Once in the airstream, the door began to peel back the skin of the airplane, opening a ten-by-twenty-foot hole in the side of the airplane triangulating to an apex at the windows of the upper deck.

"Once the storage bins were open to the night sky, baggage began to fly out of the storage area and some became ingested by the No. 3 engine, causing it to tear itself apart in a flaming belch of fire, smoke, and fumes."

The first officer informed air traffic control that the airplane was in an emergency descent and had lost power on the number 3 engine. The crew declared an emergency, and the approach 7700 emergency code was placed in the airplane's radar beacon transponder.

"The noise after the decompression was deafening. It was like if you were to lay down on a railroad track and have a freight train run over you. You could not communicate with anyone verbally; the noise was too loud. The one flight attendant in the upper deck was seat-belted in with a four-way restraint belt facing aft. Her face was ashen and her eyes were shrunken in her sockets. She was, like us, terrified. There was nothing she could do either.

"Oxygen masks had deployed from the overhead compartment as advertised, however, there was no oxygen flowing. We learned later that the oxygen bottles which fed the passenger oxygen system had blown out of the aircraft at decompression. I then saw flames shooting out of both the intake and exhaust of the No. 3 engine. No! Now we are on fire too! Shortly thereafter, the No. 4 engine, the second one outboard on the starboard side, had begun to flame. Not known then, but the flight crew ended up shutting down both engines on the right side and were flying on only two engines, both on the port side, creating incredible asymmetric thrust and yawing to the right.

"We never heard one word over the aircraft speaker system, the noise was too loud. The flight attendant did later begin to try and communicate with hand signals – put your mask on – but to no avail."

The second officer left the cockpit area to inspect the main deck. He was only out of the cockpit for a few minutes. The NTSB, in preparing transcripts of cockpit conversations, does not publish swear words. Instead, in the transcript, the NTSB inserts, "*** expletive deleted." Roughly, the transcript of the second officer's report to the captain upon his return was—"Expletive deleted, the expletive deleted side of the airplane is gone." To which the captain replied, "Expletive deleted, the expletive deleted the what is gone?" It doesn't take much imagination to fill in the blanks of that conversation. The second officer reported to the captain that a large portion of the forward right side of the cabin fuselage was missing. The captain subsequently shut down the number 4 engine because of visible flashes of fire.

Fortunately, this flight crew—Cronin, Slader and Thomas—did everything right. Even when they deviated from protocol, it was the right decision. This transcript and in-flight scenario was used by many airlines subsequent to this incident as a model of the proper way for a cockpit crew to work together. Crew resource management

(CRM) is what this interface is called. In flight training, CRM is affectionately referred to as charm school. The United crew on this night got it right. It could have easily been 308 dead versus nine.

"The flight attendant ran through the things she was trained to do. We all had our seatbelts on, so that was not a problem. She attempted to go through her emergency procedures, but it was impossible to communicate. The passengers began to talk back and forth with each other with hand gestures. We mouthed the words to each other, like 'we're going down!' while pointing down towards that water. The stewardess couldn't tell us to put on our masks or life vests, but she could act it out.

"She stood up and showed us where they were and pantomimed pulling them out, and then she opened one up and showed us how to put it on, and we did the same. The flight attendant was strapped in 99 percent of the time, but once or twice she unstrapped herself to demonstrate what she needed to do.

"There was a terrible dilemma because the two women seated next to the twisted, disfigured window didn't know what to do. They wanted to get away from the out-rushing air and the separation at the window. Yet there was nowhere to move to. The upper deck was full. So, they stayed where they were and leaned into their husbands and tried to get away from the hole as much as possible.

"Below, a large chunk of the main deck was missing. Ten seats with eight passengers still strapped into their seats were gone. Just gone. Ejected from the aircraft at 23,000 feet. One passenger, across the aisle was also missing. His seatbelt was unbuckled. His wife had been seated opposite him across the aisle. Whether he unstrapped in a vain attempt to help her, or was unstrapped at the time of the decompression and was blown out of his seat we will never know. The actual event happened in seconds. Too quick for anyone to react. Perhaps he was unbuckled and was blown from his still-fastened seat."

The primary damage to the airplane consisted of a hole on the right side in the area of the forward-facing cargo door, approximately ten-by-fifteen feet large. The cargo door fuselage frame was still intact, but the door was missing. A large section of the fuselage skin measuring about thirteen feet lengthwise by fifteen feet vertically and extending from the cargo doorframe to the upper deck windows was stripped away. One upper deck window was partially twisted out.

"When the decompression happened, the cabin filled with debris. Everything that wasn't tied down became airborne. Papers, pens, books, magazines. I lost my watch. There was a fine dust in the air from separated torn plastic that got in your eyes and nose and mouth. I remember ducking down, below the seat back to stay out of the airflow. At that point I felt I had a very short time to live. You think of all the things you should have done. I thought about my son, Seth. He lived with his mother. Seth, only ten at the time, was always worried about me when I traveled. He would worry and I wouldn't. He used to say I should be careful because I am always around airplanes – private, general aviation, and commercial – always flying somewhere. After I left, he told me to have a safe flight. I thought of him. I pictured him in the best light that I could and just wished I could have held him and hugged him one more time.

"People often ask me, 'did you think you were going to die?' I say, 'No. I knew I was going to die!' When I saw the fire in the engine, I felt the airplane pitch down in a descent and felt the decompression. I did not believe a commercial 747 could continue to fly with that much damage.

"The folks in business class in the main deck had it much worse. The remaining passengers were staring out into the dark sky and stars and black ocean. Seats, filled with people, fellow travelers, only moments before were gone. Disappeared into the void of space. The force of the rushing air made communication impossible. One passenger, Paul Hotz, from Sydney, was traveling with his wife, young daughter, and executive assistant. His wife was in the last seat adjacent to the departed row. Right next to the hole. The void.

"He covered his young daughter with a blanket and reached for his wife. He then noticed a female flight attendant struggling on the floor in the aisle next to him. Paul, a competitive kickboxer and martial arts fighter, reached out with his legs and wrapped them around the young woman, holding her in place so she would not be sucked out of the aircraft. She remained locked in the life death grip until landing.

"Time was suspended. I couldn't tell you if it was 20 seconds, 20 minutes, or 20 hours, that the plane droned on. However, after a while, I remember clearly hearing, even over the horrifying rush of noise, the steady drone of at least one engine. I knew both engines on the right side were shut down due to fires. I thought to myself, 'this bucket of bolts is still flying, we're not going to crash right now.' Because as bad as it was, as noisy as it was, we still had structural integrity. Still, I was petrified that another hunk of fuselage would break away and fly off. If a part of the plane hit the tail, it would be all over. I knew too much about aviation accidents and the compounding effects of problems which normally lead to catastrophe.

"Secondly, in the back of my mind, I kept thinking there would be an impact – us hitting the water. It's like when you're in a car and someone else is driving erratically. You keep putting your foot on the imaginary brake because you don't know if they will. I kept curling up my toes and pushing my feet into the floor because I felt like I didn't know how hard we were going to hit. Were we going to die? Roll over? Would there be water coming in? I curled up my toes because if you're going to hit, you want to be ready for it. You want to land on your feet. Incredible crazy thoughts for an incredible time.

"In my haste to leave home in Denver, I realized I had quite a bit of room in the top of my carry-on bag. On impulse, I grabbed my snorkeling mask, snorkel and fins and stuffed them down in my carry-on. I had planned on going to the Great Barrier Reef in Australia and I thought I could do some snorkeling. In the most bizarre moment aboard United 811, for a second, I contemplated opening my carry-on, donning my mask, snorkel, and fins in case we ended up in the ocean. Unbelievable! What would the other passengers think?

"The time between the decompression and when we finally got back seemed like hours. Somebody who had a watch later on told me it was about 20 minutes. I remember turning to the guy seated next to me and shouting, 'let's get this Mother on the ground!' It was incredible to me that everything was holding together.

"Then I saw this young man from California seated on the right side of the aircraft turn from the window and mouth the words, 'Land, land! There's land!' He kept pointing outside. Intermittently, we began to see specks of light from land in the ocean. As more people noticed the lights, a ripple of applause and hand clapping above our heads could be seen from each row as they noticed the sight.

"As a pilot myself, I knew we had one major hurdle to go, and that was touchdown. Passengers on the main deck later told me that there was an announcement made: 'Two minutes to landing.' While that may have relieved them, we heard nothing.

"The flight attendant did get up and say, 'Assume the position!' You're supposed to bend over and put your head between your legs and brace for impact. It's a very dehumanizing position. If I am going to die, I want to die standing up, or at least sitting up, looking at what's going to kill me. I remember thinking of the old joke, the instructions for nuclear war: 'Bend over, put your head between your legs, and kiss your ass goodbye.'"

The airplane was cleared for an approach to HNL Runway 8L. The final approach was flown at 190 to 200 knots with the number 1 and number 2 engines only. During flap extension, the flight crew observed an indication of asymmetrical flaps as the flap position approached 5°. The flight crew decided to extend inboard trailing edge flaps to 10° for the landing. The right outboard leading-edge slat did not extend during the flap-lowering sequence. The airplane touched down on the runway, approximately one thousand feet from the approach end, and came to a stop about seven thousand feet later. The captain applied idle reverse on the number 1 and number 2 engines and employed moderate to heavy braking to stop the airplane. At 02:34 (HST), HNL tower was notified by the flight crew that the airplane was stopped, and an emergency evacuation had commenced on the runway.

"*Captain Cronin put the airplane down right on the centerline. As a pilot, as a passenger, as a victim, I give him four stars. He applied maximum braking. I know he blew some of the tires. He got the airplane stopped very quickly.*

"*As we touched down and started roll-out, the passengers had their second wave of emotional outpouring. We felt we made it. People started to yell and clap and they had big grins on their faces, and we were all giving our thumbs-up again because we still couldn't hear each other. When I got downstairs to the main deck, I finally saw the amount of airplane skin and fuselage that was missing. When I saw that gaping hole, the one you could drive a truck through, I said 'Oh my God! I'm glad I could not see that while we were airborne.'*

"*And then it was that quick. That inflated slide is one fast ride out of an airplane. You come down that thing like a son of gun. As I hit the bottom of the slide, a rescue person grabbed me beneath the armpits. As I was struggling to my feet, somebody else came down and hit me in the small of the back. I got out of there. It wasn't until I got outside and stood on the tarmac that what I'd been through really hit me. My arms got weak and I started to shiver. I felt like my whole body was slowly being lowered inch-by-inch into a pool of ice water. The adrenaline was wearing off and I realized I was going into shock. At that time, I don't think any of us, with the exception of those who'd been closest to the blowout, knew there had been fatalities. We thought we had all mercifully survived a very close call.*

"*The joy we had felt for surviving turned to sorrow and mourning for our fellow passengers.*

"There is nothing so arbitrary as an aviation accident. It's such a random cross-section of humanity. Why had I been spared? What or who decided who would live and who would die? Yes, we survived, but not without guilt.

"I have said before this accident, many times, that nobody can go through an experience like this and not have it have a profound effect on his life. I think I really believe that now. I think I have been changed. I'm not so naive as to say I'm going to take time to smell the roses and enjoy life a little bit more, because that's what got me into this thing. It was the very vacation that I talked myself into thinking I needed that got me on that airplane; but I do feel that, having had an experience like this, I've got a much closer empathy for those who have grieved, who have lost and suffered similar experiences. It's probably raised my humanity quotient a notch. 'But why does it take a disaster and the threat of death to bring people together?'"

Here some passengers died, and this man, my partner, was spared. In fact, in this case, the vast majority of the passengers did survive. It is of some value to hear the thoughts of passengers on a large jet airliner where the majority of the passengers survived but thought they were going to die, and others died. The effect on these survivors varies substantially from person-to-person. The fear, anxiety, mental anquish, and other non-physical and non-economic damage are valuable data for both design engineers and lawyers.

Unfortunately, the cases arising out of United Airlines Flight 811 were never tried in court on liability. The defendants admitted liability on issues such as product liability for the aircraft design and negligence in operation and inspection of the airplane, the door fasteners, electrical circuits, and crew warning systems. Only the damages of the passengers were tried or settled.

The subject 747 was repaired and put back in service. The airplane was one of the initial 747s built by Boeing, designated as a B-747-122. At the time of this rapid explosive decompression, the aircraft had been flown for more than 58,000 hours. The weight at takeoff was 706,000 pounds, and it was carrying a flight crew of 3, a cabin crew of 15, and 337 passengers.

The safety and structural integrity of doors on very large, wide-body airliners had been a concern right from the beginning. The very large area of these doors used in a pressurized compartment resulted in huge forces wanting to blow the door out. For example, if we had a door that was fifteen-by-ten feet like we had on the subject 747, and a pressurization of approximately 9 psi (pounds per square inch), the force wanting to open the door would be near 200,000 pounds.

United and other airlines have had issues with the integrity of such doors on previous occasions.

Both the latches and structural integrity of the doors are at issue. Most of the entrance doors are now plug doors that are held in a close position by the pressurization rather than relying on latches. Maybe all pressurized openings should be plugs.

It would have been advantageous to have had a jury trial on the product liability issues. We could have had the design of the door structure, the latches, the electrical circuits, and the crew cockpit warning issues evaluated and debated by expert witnesses, plus the court and the jury viewing demonstrative evidence, like pictures, videos, and models.

The admitted liability settlements are most often with nondisclosure agreements. The goal is to protect the airplane, engines, and system's brand by keeping the problems out of the media and other chat platforms.

CHAPTER 11

United Airlines Flight 232

The plane shook back and forth
The passengers screamed in horror
Thousands of feet in the air
There will be no tomorrow

—*Frank Del*

August 12, 1985

Japan Airlines Flight 123 climbed out of Tokyo's Haneda Airport at 6:04 p.m. local time. The Boeing 747SR aircraft was bound for Osaka with 524 souls onboard. Twelve minutes after takeoff, the Boeing underwent a rapid decompression when an improperly repaired bulkhead suffered a structural failure, destroying much of the empennage (tail section). As a result, all of the ship's hydraulic systems were damaged. In an instant, Captain Masami Takahama lost his primary and secondary flight controls. All that remained for controlling the airplane was the thrust of the four engines.

The crew then struggled for approximately one-half hour attempting to steer and control the airplane by manipulating the engine thrust before the 747 crashed into Osutaka Ridge in Gunma Prefecture. Of the 524 occupants, only 4 survived. The crash became the largest loss of life from a single aircraft accident in history. It still is today.

The primary and secondary flight controls on most jet airline transports are hydraulically actuated. That is, hydraulic fluid is pressed on by the controls in the cockpit, resulting in the transmission of forces to actuators that move the control surfaces such as elevator, rudder, aileron, flaps, and slats. Though they've been used this way in the past, jet engines are there to provide thrust and not flight control. Therefore, pilots are not trained to use the engines to control the airplane. It's not very effective and is dangerous.

However, if all flight controls have been rendered useless, intuition tells a very good pilot that the engines may be of some use. It's kind of your last shot when you are driving a broken airplane weighing hundreds of thousands of pounds and full of passengers. By changing the thrust, the speed can be changed, and because of that, the airplane can be made to climb and descend and also to turn. However, there's also the risk that by increasing speed, damaged parts could be torn off the plane or that, by decreasing speed, the airplane may stall and fall from the sky. By the same token, differential thrust can steer the airplane, but this may also cause stability and control problems. The big problem is the pilot flying with engine control only doesn't really know what might happen. It is a tricky and dangerous scenario.

So, when flight instructor Captain Dennis Fitch jumped onto United Airlines Flight 232 from Denver to Chicago late one afternoon two years after the devastating crash of Japan Airlines Flight 123, he was likely one of the few pilots on the planet who had practiced flying and landing a large jet airplane using thrust only for control.

Incidentally, he learned of the crash of the Boeing 747 in Japan not long after it occurred and was taken with the idea that the crew had attempted to control the plane solely by manipulating engine power. At this time, Denny was a flight simulator instructor at United Airlines based in Denver, and he had taken it upon himself to practice the technique in the simulator.

Denny had worked for United Airlines since 1968 and had about twenty thousand hours of flight time, which meant he was a veteran. Working for United, he enjoyed the perk of a free pass to catch a ride on an air carrier.

On this day, July 19, 1989, he was flying to Chicago from Denver's Stapleton International Airport. He had passed up the chance to board another flight that left five minutes earlier. When asked why he had waited to fly on Flight 232, he didn't have an answer. His decision, however, would prove crucial. Later, he noted to the media, "I was forty-six years old. I had the whole world ahead of me. I was a captain for a major U.S. airline. I had a beautiful healthy family, a loving wife, and a great future. At four o'clock that day, I was just trying to stay alive."

The flight left Stapleton International Airport as scheduled, at 14:09 Mountain Daylight Time, and climbed uneventfully to its cruising altitude of thirty-nine thousand feet. A little over an hour into the flight, there was a loud bang in the rear of the plane, and the airframe began to shudder and vibrate. The crew quickly realized that the number 2 engine had failed. But the McDonnell Douglas DC-10 was a three-engine airplane, and the number 2 engine was mounted in the center, so its loss should not have been a big issue. In fact, one engine inoperative was not even on the emergency checklist then. It was merely considered an abnormal condition.

The crew may have thought that the noise was just a compressor stall as the engine was flaming out. Airline crews are trained for such events. If that is all that happened, the flight would have just continued on to Chicago's O'Hare Airport with little trouble.

But this was more than just an engine failure. The titanium stage 1 fan disk on the number 2 engine had come apart, taking a substantial portion of the front of the engine with it. The disk, which burst, held the fan blades. These are the blades that you see when you look into the front of a jet engine—the ones that you might hear rattling when a turbojet engine is shutting down. These blades are attached to a disk that spins about 4,000 RPM while the tips of the blades are going at near supersonic speed. This rotating fan is required by regulatory laws to have a retaining ring to prevent rotating parts from flying out and creating havoc and causing damage to other airplane systems.

Back in the cabin, the passengers knew that something had gone terribly wrong. Several passengers thought a bomb had exploded. One of the senior flight attendants thought there had been a breach in the structure of the fuselage and that the cabin would depressurize, sucking out everything that wasn't fastened down. There were also several babies-in-arms that day. It was "children's day," a special offered by United Airlines. However, nothing seemed to be flying around the cabin, and although everyone was scared, the situation seemed to stabilize.

Shortly thereafter, Captain Haynes spoke through the cabin speakers. With a calm and reassuring voice, he informed passengers that the airplane had experienced an engine failure but assured all aboard that the DC-10 was very capable of flying safely on the two remaining engines.

These words were hardly out of Captain Haynes mouth when the airplane's right wing dipped, and the plane seemed to be rolling to the right. The flight crew didn't yet know the full extent of the damage, but they were now aware that they were losing control of the aircraft. The first officer, William Records, confirmed this after he tried to take control from his side of the cockpit.

The airplane was still flying but losing altitude and turning to the right—the direction the plane was turning at the time the number 2 engine blew apart. Captain Haynes stabilized the aircraft by reducing power on the number 1 engine and began to run a check to figure out what they were facing.

He then called the senior flight attendant to the cockpit to have her prepare the passengers for an emergency landing. At the same time, the crew called Minneapolis Center as they were handling the in-route air-traffic control east of Denver. Flight 232 requested emergency assistance.

It was then that Denny Fitch, seated in first class, motioned to a flight attendant. He explained that he was a flight simulator instructor and also a captain for United and was willing to help if the captain wished.

She relayed the message to Captain Haynes. "Let 'em come up" was how he responded. His voice was captured on the cockpit voice recorder.

As Fitch entered the cockpit, the crew was still sorting out their loss of controls.

"We don't have any flight controls," said Haynes, who then sent Denny back into the cabin to visually check the wings and anything else he could inspect in the way of damage or any unusual condition.

Just then, the first officer is heard asking a key question, "What's the total hydraulic quantity?"

"Zero," the second officer replied.

"On all of them?"

The crew was now realizing that they were in a "world of hurt." It was hard to imagine that they could make it to a runway or, for that matter, to an airport.

Fitch returned from the cabin and explained that the right-side inboard ailerons were stuck in an up position. This explained the tendency for the right wing to drop and the plane wanting to turn right. It was then that Captain Haynes gave Fitch the critical assignment that would determine how and when this flight would end. He asked him to take control of the power levers. This job would require both hands, one on each lever. His doing so would free the pilots for other tasks.

It was the manipulation of the power levers of the number 1 and number 3 engines that would decide the fate of everyone onboard. The only way the airplane could climb, descend, turn, or change speed was through the use of these two levers. None of this was predictable, but the job had to be done by only one dedicated person. As it was, Captain Haynes was unaware that he had the best man for the job.

The plane had also developed a phugoid mode oscillation. This is an instability mode that results in the airplane pitching up and down. It will continually climb and descend, looking much like the sine wave that you might recall from high school trigonometry. This was another problem that Denny was trying to mitigate with the power levers.

Not long after Denny took the levers, Minneapolis Air Traffic Control suggested an emergency landing at Sioux Gateway Airport in Iowa. "You are cleared to land on any runway," the controller reported.

"You want to be particular and make it a runway, huh?" Captain Haynes was heard to say. His joke betrays what kind of shape they were in.

Captain Haynes then called the senior flight attendant to the cockpit again and explained what was happening. He told her they were going to have a difficult landing and that as they prepared for impact, he would give the passengers the warning of, "Brace, brace, brace!"

She left the cockpit and began preparing the passengers. Now they were about seven miles from the airport. A few minutes later, the captain gave the passengers a two-minute warning. There was no turning back. They were committed. It had been almost forty-five minutes since the number 2 engine had self-destructed. The passengers and the crew had this time to contemplate their fate.

Fitch manipulated the throttles all the way to the ground, but just before they hit, Captain Haynes is heard saying, "Close the throttles."

Fitch responded, "I can't pull them off, or we'll lose it. That's what's turning ya." Although seconds from the crash landing and descending about three times the normal rate and about one hundred knots faster than a normal stabilized approach to landing, Fitch had a feel for the situation. He knew that if he came off the throttles, at that moment, he would kill everyone onboard. He had worked the levers with everything he had. For all his efforts, almost unbelievably, considering the plane's condition, the nose was pointed to the numbers on the approach end of the runway.

They touched down almost in the center of runway 22. But, the right wing hit before the landing gear, and the plane skidded in that direction and toppled into an inverted position; it then cartwheeled across the airport field. With fuel in the air and on the ground, there was a tremendous explosion. Smoke and fire inhalation claimed the largest number of lives. One hundred and eleven people died. But one hundred eighty-five, including the entire crew, survived even though the cockpit broke away from the fuselage and bounced across the airport like a ball.

Various people on the ground had known that this crippled United flight was going to attempt an emergency landing in Sioux City about fifteen minutes ahead of time. As a result, they videoed the approach and crash. The video showed that the aircraft broke up into three primary pieces. Because the cockpit had ripped off from the front part of the fuselage, the first-class section was opened and totally exposed. Few of the first-class passengers lived. The main fuselage to just aft of the wing root was in one big piece. The third piece was the aft section of the fuselage and tail.

One of my over forty clients, Brad Griffin, was seated in seat 3B. He was not found until the day after the crash, when he was spotted near death in an adjacent cornfield. He had been seated in first class and had been thrown up and out of the fireball and into the field two hundred yards away. He reported that when he was airborne, he looked down into the fireball and thought, *If I go in that fire, I'll be a dead man.*

When I first met him, he was in a full-body cast. His wife, Cheryl, had retained me. Brad was on his way to Kalamazoo, Michigan. He was hoping to beat his younger brother at golf for the first time and was practiced and ready. It would be quite a while before he'd play golf after Sioux City. He ended up being one of my very best friends. He always putted with the bent putter that he had with him that day and was later found in the wreckage. It was his good luck club.

Truthfully, it was more of a crash than a landing, but making it to the approach end of the runway at all, or even near to it, and keeping the wreckage on airport property was quite a feat in itself. No FAA simulation replaying the conditions of Flight 232 ever made it to the runway. One thing was for sure, despite the normal pressure from the insurance underwriters to put the blame on pilot error, and trust me, they would have, this flight crew had outperformed all expectations.

Plaintiff's Steering Committee

What came next was to find out the details of what caused the engine to self-destruct. This part was always my passion and self-assigned mission, even beyond what I needed to do for my clients.

But initially, we had client issues. Some families would contact us directly after the crash, while other cases would come as referrals from estate attorneys, corporate attorneys, or other lawyers who realized that these cases were unique and not within their field. Then there was the choice of venue and whether the case would be best in state or federal court. This would include legal forum shopping for a court system that would provide the greatest compensation for the victims and their families. When the choice was federal court, it was important to make sure that I would be appointed to the plaintiff's steering committee, which was imperative for public relations and negotiations with the likely referring attorneys. Generally, the referring attorneys were more adept at getting clients than they would be at handling cases of this nature, which meant that if they wanted to do anything other than settle with an airline or manufacturer for a relatively low number, they needed to find an attorney who specialized in airplane crash cases. Generally, this meant these lawyers contacted my office, or one of our true competitors.

This was good for our firm since having more clients helped in many ways, including influence with the court and of course financing the case. Finding themselves in a bind, many of these clients had fallen into the offices of some pretty good marketers. They deserved a firm who could actually benefit their case.

Up until the late seventies, lawyers were not permitted to advertise. Even after the United States Supreme Court ruled that advertising was protected by the First Amendment, I still didn't advertise except to publish a newsletter that I called the *Legal Eagle* and only sent to lawyers. My cases generally came from media coverage of jury verdicts, referrals (often from estate and corporate lawyers), appearances on television, news coverage of airplane crashes, and articles published in journals and magazines.

Once advertising was allowed, the floodgates for swindlers opened and a great number of charlatans started to represent themselves as hotshot aviation disaster lawyers. They would hustle cases, approaching families in mourning and distress, selling themselves, and signing up contingent fee contracts. Their goal was to get big settlements quickly. Most of the time, the insurance companies would blow them off, at which point these charlatans would come to us and try to make a deal. This was another source that added to our client list.

United Airlines had its principal place of business in Chicago. In addition to United being a common carrier responsible for the safety of their passengers, they also inspected and overhauled their own engines. The engine overhaul shop was in San Francisco, which meant that this location was a possible venue. However, I was quite sure that the multidistrict litigation panel would assign the case to Chicago as there were a lot of aggressive law firms, some quite good, in the windy city already chasing cases.

As it turned out, these Chicago firms were concerned about my firm being the firm of choice because so many of the passengers were from Colorado and also because I was a member of both the Colorado and Illinois bars, making me an obvious contender. But, if they had any thought of blocking us, I had another card to play: a political one.

A couple of years back in the spring, my wife, Kathleen, and our two youngest kids, Scotty and Danny, and I had departed the Bahamas in our sailing ketch for New York. When we sighted the east coast of the U.S., we decided to duck into the Savannah River and spend a night in Hilton Head. After securing our mooring lines, the four of us took a few golf clubs and some balls out on the course, which was adjacent to the seawall.

There we met a friendly young man out on the fairway also hitting balls around with his son. When I asked him where he was from, he replied, "Chicago."

Kathleen said, "Oh, the last great bastion of crooked politics."

"Don't give crooked politics a bad name," he responded. "I'm a third-generation beneficiary."

He went on to add, "If you ever have any problems in Chicago, be sure to call me." I kept his card.

I had no intention of calling him. Directly after the crash, one of the first tasks was to look at the various possible forums in which I could get jurisdiction over at least one of the potential defendants. I liked the law in Illinois, but there I would have all the Chicago lawyers to deal with. On the other hand, I wanted to be on the plaintiff's steering committee, which for sure would end up in federal court in Chicago. After extensive analysis of the various possibilities, I decided to file the wrongful death cases in state court in St. Louis, Missouri. This was the principal place of business of McDonnell

Douglas before they were acquired by Douglas Airplane Company. There seemed to be enough nexus to maintain jurisdiction in the city and county of St. Louis. It also helped that the state of Missouri had a great wrongful death statute favoring plaintiffs.

I also filed a few injury cases in federal court in Chicago and was appointed to the plaintiff's steering committee. This was over the attempt on part of the Chicago lawyers to block my application. I'm not sure it was necessary, but I put a call into the gentleman whom I had met on the golf course in Hilton Head a few years prior. He simply sat in the back of the courtroom during the arguments, and it was obvious that the judge knew him. Did that help? Who knows.

Containment Ring

The defendants in all cases were United Airlines, General Electric (the engine manufacturer), and Aluminum Company of America (the supplier of the titanium).

At first it wasn't clear why the engine had come apart. It seemed most likely a fan blade had made contact with the containment ring, which caused disintegration, or that some damage had gone unnoticed, leading to the explosion. However, there was no definitive evidence to settle the question as the entire fan disk and the majority of the containment ring was lost somewhere over Iowa.

Then one afternoon, a farmer in Alta, Iowa, discovered a large piece of the disk in his field. The rest of it was found not far away. Investigators further discovered the top portion of the containment ring nearby. Analysis began immediately.

The NTSB investigative team was made up of members of the airlines and the manufacturers. These types of investigative teams always concern plaintiff's lawyers for the simple fact that the parties lean toward protecting themselves, their brands, and products, and although the insurance companies are not permitted to actively participate, they seem to always have a phantom effect on the results and conclusions. It's also of note that no one from the plaintiff's steering committee participates in the investigative process because they are assumed to have a bias that would affect the results and conclusions.

Notwithstanding this paradox, the investigation of Flight 232 was pretty accurate, though I've known several that were not.

As it turned out, the titanium disk, which held the blades of the first rotating part in the engine inlet called the fan, had a microscopic metallurgical defect, which caused fatigue cracking, which grew until the centrifugal force caused it to fly apart, taking the containment ring with it. This disk was made of a forged titanium alloy, with a 32-inch diameter, weighing some 370 pounds and manufactured by Aluminum Company of America. As light and strong as titanium is, the process of manufacturing is extensive and complex. It is understandable that metallurgical flaws might result.

In this case, the titanium billet from which the disk was machined had a microscopic defect in the metal. The defect was a very small inclusion of a particle that was inconsistent with the structure of the intended titanium alloy. This teeny-weeny particle set off a chain reaction that brought the plane down. The billet with the defect slipped past all the inspection procedures. However, a complete inspection of the billet, using all proper procedures in place at the time, would have discovered this inclusion.

Notwithstanding this microscopic, non-metallic inclusion, should such a failure have ended in this horrible disaster?

The answer is no!

If the containment ring had contained the shrapnel as it was designed to, then the flight controls wouldn't have been totally lost, and the plane would have landed with little difficulty. Furthermore, if the hydraulic lines had been properly placed, then the flight controls wouldn't have been lost either. If there had been a proper alternate hydraulic system, then the crew could have safely landed the airplane. The required design standards dictate that there should be no "single point of failure that will result in loss of an aircraft," but that clearly hadn't been the case with this design.

My task was to make the defects in design and manufacturing, as well as the negligence in quality assurance and inspection, clear, thus causing public pressure to force the necessary changes. This is where large jury verdicts were more effective in causing design changes and changes in the manufacturing processes than I could ever accomplish as a young in-house engineer.

My death cases filed in St. Louis were settled on the courthouse steps on the day set for trial. The families of the decedents were well-compensated.

Later, the plaintiff's steering committee settled the remainder of the cases in federal court in Chicago for significant sums.

CHAPTER 12

Flight Without A Fin

*Ease the yoke and now the rudder, the
trick is not to make her shudder*

—*Patrick J. Phillips*

"Rudder to the Fire Wall"

Test pilot Charlie Fisher was flying a U.S. Air Force B52H bomber north along the front range of the Rockies from New Mexico to Colorado. He was paralleling the Sangre de Cristo mountains to the west.

With a crew of three, he had flown from Boeing's military headquarters on McConnell Air Force Base in Wichita, Kansas, at an altitude of five hundred feet above ground level. They turned north upon reaching the Rockies where they were conducting the sixth leg of a test mission.

It was January 1964, the height of the Cold War, and flying a bomber of this size at such low altitudes was a tactic designed to avoid new Russian air defenses. This bomber was originally designed for high-altitude bombing missions and was aptly named the "Stratofortress." This particular aircraft was on loan from the Air Force as part of a military contract under which Boeing was to collect fatigue and gust load stress data. Engineers were concerned about the unique stresses that would be experienced flying so close to the ground. The craft was fully instrumented with about six hundred strain gauges, accelerometers, and the necessary recording equipment.

Near Wagon Mound, New Mexico, the flight encountered turbulent forces high enough that Charlie abandoned the test and began climbing. A bit above fourteen thousand feet, slightly east of Colorado's East Spanish Peak, the plane encountered what a Boeing report said were "the combined effects of a [wind] rotor associated with a mountain wave and lateral shear." As co-pilot Richard Curry puts it, the plane encountered "rapid, explosive like gust" of turbulence. These struck the aircraft from the right, pitching the plane upward and causing it to yaw to the left. The plane was then struck from the left, resulting in "a very rapid yaw to the right and a resultant right rolling movement." The event lasted nine seconds. The crew felt a vibration in the controls, and navigator James Pittman, then stationed on the plane's lower deck, was thrown over the nav table into the left side of the plane.

In Charlie Fisher's words, "During the second portion of the encounter, the airplane's motion actually seemed to be negating my control inputs. I had the rudder to the fire wall, the column in my lap and full wheel, and I wasn't having any luck righting the airplane."

Since the rudder doesn't actually have a fire wall, what Fisher meant was that he had pushed the B52 controls to the limits in order to regain flight control, which he was able to achieve. But for a moment, Fisher thought he had lost all control and ordered the crew to prepare to bail out. Quickly, however, they realized the plane could still fly, yet something was wrong.

It wasn't until an F-100 Super Sabre fighter jet was scrambled to get a visual that the crew understood what had happened. Almost the entire vertical stabilizer, some 95 percent had been torn off the B52. It had broken off in a ragged manner, leaving jagged pieces of aluminum structure sticking up from the rear end of the fuselage. It was then that the iconic photograph of the Stratofortress flying without a vertical tail was taken.

After righting the plane, the crew immediately thought of returning to Wichita, but the high winds in Kansas and the denser population around the base would have made landing without the stabilizer an unacceptable risk. Instead, they were re-routed to Blytheville Air Force Base in Arkansas where the conditions were better. A KC-135 (an in-flight fuel tanker) full of Boeing engineers followed them en route.

All told, the crew flew for five hours in their broken B52. Not long afterward, the Air Force made a classified instructional film. They entitled it *Flight without a Fin*.

Although I had left Boeing at the time the film was available, I was made aware of it because I was close to many of the flight test crews flying out of McConnell Air Force Base and had been an engineer on the project.

In this instance, the vertical stabilizer structure was highly fatigued from its gust load history, and the pilot had done whatever he thought necessary to keep the plane flying under the circumstances. The mission was to intentionally fly outside the structural design flight envelope. It wasn't too surprising then that they broke the airplane. But no one ever questioned Charlie's actions or what he claimed he had done with the plane when he said that he "had the rudder to the fire wall, the column in his lap, and full wheel." This was the first time I remember the vertical stabilizer of an airplane simply coming off in flight.

Charlie received a lot of kudos, and everyone I talked to thought Fisher did only what he had to recover the aircraft and to save lives. The same can hardly be said about the treatment received by the seasoned co-pilot of an American Airlines flight that crashed into Belle Harbor, New York, on November 12, 2001. But unlike Charlie, this pilot never lived to defend himself.

Airbus A300 and the NTSB

American Airlines Flight 587 was bound for Santo Domingo in the Dominican Republic and departing from JFK in New York. The first officer, Sten Molin, was the flying pilot that day when the Airbus encountered the wake vortex of a Japan Airlines 747 just after takeoff.

As he struggled to right the airplane, the vertical stabilizer separated from the rear of the fuselage, and the Airbus broke apart over Long Island, raining down into the bay and onto homes and roadways in Queens. Its crash led to the second-highest loss of life in United States history.

As this incident also involved the detachment of the airplane's vertical stabilizer, comparisons with the B52 are natural, but on this occasion, the tail seemed to break cleanly off the fuselage, a sight that most people had never seen. While in the case of the B52, "the flight without a fin," the empennage was looked at in-flight by the pilot flying the F-100 and later on the ground by teams of engineers and test pilots from both the United States Air Force and Boeing. The tail being torn off the B52 was not so shocking as that of American

Airlines Flight 587. It was fairly clear that the tail broke off as a result of a series of fatigue failures. (Much like bending a coat hanger back and forth until it breaks.)

Also, the structure of the B52 was a much different design both in terms of materials and geometry. The B52 architecture was what engineers would refer to as a semi-monocoque structure, that is, where the loads of the tail were carried partially by aluminum ribs and spars and partially by the aluminum skin, a design that had been around since the days of yore. On the other hand, the Airbus had a new type of structure on which the fittings attaching the spars to the fuselage were made of a composite or "plastic" material. In the mid-1980s, the industry was experimenting with replacing some of the aluminum structural parts of aircraft structure with non-metallic composites. Over the last thirty years or so, these composites have evolved and changed a bunch. The material used for the tail of the A300 Airbus at issue was somewhat early in the evolution process. It was referred to as carbon fiber-reinforced plastic (CFRP). These composite materials have come a long way since. They are now quite stronger, lighter, and much more consistent in the manufacturing process.

At the time of Flight 587, the use of composite aircraft structures was somewhat a rarity in airliners. This type of in-flight structural failure was also very rare, if not unheard of.

The crash raised a lot of questions among pilots and engineers. The NTSB itself, in its final report on the crash, agreed that the separation of the vertical tail here was something new and of great concern when they wrote, "The in-flight separation of the vertical stabilizer from the fuselage of a transport-category airplane is an extremely rare, if not an unprecedented, occurrence." Justifiably, there seemed to be questions concerning the integrity of these relatively new composites.

But as the story of Flight 587's crash unfolded we would see the investigation leaning away from questioning the structural integrity of the tail. And we started to see the flight's first officer have his good name and record questioned in releases to the media based on a prior very minor single incident where his performance had been criticized and never reported at the time it was said to have occurred. Other than that one incident, this pilot was referred to several times as exceptional and excellent.

With this crash coming as it did so close on the heels of the September 11 Twin Towers terrorist attacks, the story garnered even more attention than it might have otherwise. There was a great deal of speculation that this mass air disaster was in fact an attack.

Again, there was talk of a streak of light in the sky. But, the cockpit voice recorder and flight data recorder recovered not long after the crash proved otherwise. The NTSB almost three years later would write in their report, "The probable cause of this accident was the in-flight separation of the vertical stabilizer as a result of the loads beyond the ultimate design that were created by the first officer's unnecessary and excessive rudder pedal inputs. Contributing to these rudder pedal inputs were the characteristics of the A300-600 rudder system design and elements of the American Airlines Advanced Aircraft Maneuvering Program."

What they described was a perfect storm of sorts: sensitive rudder inputs, erroneous training in rudder use, and a pilot with an aggressive rudder history. This history was way overstated.

So far as it goes, what the Board's report had stated was factual. The vertical stabilizer had encountered loads beyond its design parameters and broke off, and yes, the pilot was using the rudder pedals at the time it broke. Further, he had been trained in a certain way to use the rudders. The A300 rudder controls also happen to be particularly sensitive. That much is clear. But the way in which the vertical stabilizer broke off, that is, cleanly when one of the composite attach fittings broke, and with the airplane flying below maneuvering speed, indicates that the report ignored a basic issue. Yes, they talk about the carbon fiber fitting, but in a rather sophomoric way.

Maneuvering speed is a specified limitation, represented by V_A. The use of the flight controls to the stops below this speed should not overload the structural strength of the airplane. Also, when I read that the fittings that broke were all made of non-metallic composites, and on previous models none of the corresponding Airbus metal fittings had broken, I started to seriously consider whether a carbon fiber-reinforced plastic attach fitting might be the cause of the crash.

I remember seeing footage of the almost nearly intact vertical stabilizer as it was retrieved from Jamaica Bay by the Army Corp. of Engineers. The broken parts looked so clean, like the tail had fallen off a delivery truck rather than having just broken off an airliner in-flight. From the images, it appeared that this fin had come off right at its attach points like a toy model airplane after a child had broken off the wing.

Airplane structures were initially wood and fabric. As they became bigger and faster machines, materials changed. By the time of World War II and through the beginning of the jet age, air transports were using aluminum as the primary structural material. Aluminum alloys worked well for so many reasons. It was homogeneous, a light metal, and used successfully throughout many other industries. Aluminum alloys had also been tested for years. We knew its strength and its fatigue life, and it was relatively easy to protect from corrosion.

But things must evolve. Boats that had been made of plywood and aluminum were being replaced with fiberglass and other plastic-like compounds. These synthetic and semi-synthetic compounds were malleable and could foreseeably be quite light and made strong. It was beginning to look like such composites had a place in building airframes. It wasn't long before we saw airplane designers using composite material for secondary structure and trim. Such materials as fiberglass or carbon fibers were held together in a matrix of epoxy resin. Other branded plastics like Kevlar became popular for airframe filets, shaping contours, and for wing tips.

As was inevitable, these composites began to play a major role in aerodynamic surfaces, controls, and attach points as well.

My concern was that these new composites were developing and changing so rapidly that it was nearly impossible to collect any historical test data, such as accurate breaking strength or fatigue life. Not only were the formulas for the resin and fibers changing rapidly, the materials were laid up and fabricated in ever-changing geometric patterns. Accordingly, it was very difficult to establish a baseline for strength and performance.

An example of the problem is reflected in the rig on my sailing ketch. This vessel had a very high center of gravity because of the quantity of steel rod in the rigging. This made the boat very tender (tippy). At a point in time, I calculated that I could take about eight thousand pounds out of the rig by replacing much of the steel rod with non-metallic composite stays and shrouds. I did this, but ever since then, when we've had a failure and looked into replacing a piece of the composite rigging, we learned that the current composite made by the same company had changed. So, we are never dealing with the same material as we did originally.

More to the point, Airbus is not currently using the same composite materials as they were at the time that the non-metallic attach point broke in Flight 587. Yet the commonly used metal alloys of steel and aluminum have been the same for years and years. We are pretty confident we know the ultimate tensile, compressive, and shear strength of these metals. Additionally, and of great importance, they have an established fatigue life.

After the crash, and as the weeks and months passed, it seemed as if the investigation continued in earnest. I was involved in doing the legal work for the victims' families, most of whom resided in the Dominican Republic. I had been polishing up my bad Spanish from the days after having sunk my boat off the north shore of Cuba. Spanish was the primary language of most of the surviving families and their local lawyers. Yet interestingly enough, French was the language of law in the D.R. Here, I needed a lot of help. In that regard, I spent some time at the law school at Pontificia Universidad Católica Madre Y Maestra (Mother and Teacher Pontifical Catholic University) located in Santiago, Dominican Republic. On the campus, I met several lawyers with whom I worked on local probate matters arising out of the wrongful death cases.

There was a remarkable aspect to the Dominican death case. Under the wrongful death law of the Dominican Republic, not only were spouses able to make a claim for damages but also significant others. This came into play because several of the passengers maintained homes in both the northeast of the U.S. and the D.R. I had both sweethearts and wives making claims for wrongful death damages for the same passenger.

During this time, the liability seemed obvious. I looked at it as a product liability case against the airplane designer and manufacturer, namely, Airbus. After all, the tail had broken off during very foreseeable flight conditions. I was looking forward to re-engineering the empennage structural design in the courtroom and through the media if necessary. The examination and cross-examination of engineering expert witnesses would be tantamount to a blue-ribbon structural design team, not hampered by marketing and economic pressures.

But apparently, I was a bit naive. From whispers in the media, this was beginning to smell like a pilot error case. More and more, it started to look like certain forces were steering the Flight 587 crash in the direction of blaming the flight crew, even though the industry magazines and periodicals seemed to still share my view that a structural defect was a primary cause.

In my mind, the airplane was flying below maneuvering speed (V_A), the speed below which pilots are taught that you can do almost anything with the flight controls without breaking the airplane. To this point, a *New York Times* article written by Matthew Wald and Al Baker, appearing a week after the crash expressed this very view. They wrote, "There is not supposed to be any rudder movement a pilot can command that will rip off the tail." The authors then argue, "And more so than Boeing planes, Airbus touts that it protects the pilots from their own mistakes, with automation that limits how the airplane can be maneuvered." Not only was it par for the course to assume that pilots would take aggressive action with the controls under maneuvering speed when needed, such as recovering from wake turbulence, pilots had been led to believe the Airbus was even safer than other brands. Looking back, had we all been misinformed for fifty years? I didn't think so.

Peter Garrison of the *LA Times* phrased it this way in a 2005 article, "Before the Airbus accident, nearly all pilots believed that as long as an airplane was flying at or below maneuvering speed, nothing they could do would break it." That seemed pretty straightforward. It is also what I and many others had been taught. Garrison went on to quote the FAA, saying, "That belief was universal in part because it was so logical. After all what would be the point of publishing a maneuvering speed, if it were not a safe speed for maneuvering?" Besides, the FAA explicitly supported it. The government's own *Pilot's Handbook of Aeronautical Knowledge* says, "Any combination of flight control usage [below the maneuvering speed] including full deflection of the controls...should not create an excessive air load."

Obviously, the belief was widespread and even part of flight school curriculums and regulations. Additionally, this understanding of the term was widespread enough that it constituted the meaning of the term *maneuvering speed* (V_A). If a plane's structure fails under that speed, the problem is with the structure, not with the pilot, or the term loses value.

V_A was not just a good idea but is defined in the law. Both the United States and the European Union regulatory law on airplane design set speed limitations for airplane design. The purpose of these limitations relates to airplane performance, stability and control, and most importantly to structural integrity. With regard to the specific airspeed design limitation V_A, the book states the following:

"Operating Limitations for the maneuvering speed known as V_A the law states that ... full application of rudder and aileron controls, as well as maneuvers, that involve angles of attack near the stall, should be confined to speeds below this value."

All post-crash structural analysis seemed to agree that the tail departed the fuselage because of an overload failure of the tail's rear attach point on the right side. The other five attach points followed like dominoes and the tail was gone.

I kept asking myself, *"Why? What was the motive of the NTSB for sticking to pilot error?"* A major piece of the airplane broke off during a typical departure. Wake turbulence behind another departing airplane out of JFK International Airport was not exactly rare. Airline pilots are trained to fly these planes when upset by wake turbulence. This aircraft was below maximum maneuvering speed. Yet, the investigative tide was clearly turning in the direction of pilot error as the cause of the crash of American Airlines Flight 587.

Was there some powerful force trying to defend the Airbus brand? Were their insurance underwriters applying pressure in some way? Both Airbus and American Airlines were parties to the investigation because their products were involved, and because they were parties, they were encouraged to submit their proposed findings to the NTSB before the final cause was published.

More often than not, these company employees will have a higher level of technical expertise than the Board's own employees. I have often been concerned that these highly-qualified technical employees of the manufacturers will be able to steer the Board's opinion in a direction to benefit their company and its products. I remained concerned even though there is clear regulatory law that prevents any insurer, lawyer, or potential claimant from participating as part of the NTSB investigative team.

Another wrinkle in the case is probably best described in the NTSB report. The plane's rudder controls were probably the most sensitive in the industry, and at 250 knots, the speed at which they were flying when the tail came off, it only takes a small rudder input to achieve full rudder deflection. To this last point, the A300 fleet standards manager stated that "he did not think that any pilot would have thought that full rudder could be gained from about 1 ¼ inch of pedal movement and 10 pounds of foot force [above the breakout force] at an airspeed of 250 knots."

Are the A300's sensitive rudder controls a design defect? They are if the vertical stabilizer attach fittings can break like they did below maneuvering speed. But what was the plane's maneuvering speed? The NTSB report stated that "the American Airlines A300 Operating Manual contained only one reference to design maneuvering speed [V_A], which indicated that it was the turbulence penetration speed [270 knots]." So, they were under that speed. It's worth restating, if there is a collective belief among pilots and airlines, including in FAA regulations, that under maneuvering speed, even full deflection of controls will not create "excessive air loads." The problem is not the pilots. The idea that you could do anything with the controls under maneuvering speed was just part of the way we flew.

Furthermore, the use of alternating rudder movements, which the first officer had been accused of, had been taught to pilots for decades as a procedure to force the landing gear to lock into position when they had failed to do so. If a landing gear failed to lock in the down position there would be an indication on the instrument panel by the failure to show a green okay light.

If an airplane's landing gear had not fully deployed and were stuck in an "unsafe" condition as indicated on the instrument panel, the procedure had always been to initiate a turn and then use alternating rudder inputs below maneuvering speed to force them into the down lock. This was common practice in many airplanes that I flew. It was also a procedure that had been taught to pilots for years. The procedure also happened to be listed in the 2001 *American Airlines Handbook*. The instruction read, "If one gear remains unlocked, perform turns to increase the load factor and perform alternating sideslips in an attempt to lock the gear." In other words, it told the pilot to perform a maneuver similar to the one that broke Flight 587 apart. Interestingly, this note was changed in the 2002 handbook to read, "If one gear remains unlocked, perform coordinated turns to increase the load factor [not to exceed 45 deg. of bank]."

What changed? Not fifty years of industry practice. This maneuver didn't suddenly become dangerous, and how often had it been used by pilots over the years? Had we all been in danger of breaking off our vertical stabilizer as a result of this dangerous technique in our confusion over the real meaning of maneuvering speed?

I don't believe so.

Flight 587's "probable cause" statement issued by the NTSB represents to me the clearest case of blaming the pilot at all cost, even to the point of redefining designated limitation speeds.

The question was, what actually happened up there in the skies over Queens?

The Events Leading to the Crash of Flight 587

The final moment of the flight tells the tale. These moments were captured by the cockpit voice recorder (CVR), which records sounds and voices in the cockpit, including radio transmissions; and the flight data recorder (FDR), which records physical data such as control positions, control forces, airspeed, altitude, airplane position, and many other parameters (the infamous black boxes). They give some insight into why and how the plane went down.

After waiting short of the "hold line" for some time, the tower gave them the go-ahead. Captain Ed States then informed the passengers, "At long last, we are number two for takeoff. Immediately after takeoff, we'll be in a left turn, heading for the shoreline."

Fatefully, this left turn would put them on track to be behind and below the JAL 747's new course assigned by air traffic control. The next transmission is from the tower, "American five eighty-seven heavy, Kennedy tower, caution wake turbulence, three one left, taxi into position and hold." The wake turbulence of concern were the vortices that were being shed from the wing tips of the JAL 747.

These vortices are like little tornadoes that result from the lift of the preceding airplane's wing. Thus, the heavier the airplane, the greater the lift required and normally the greater the strength of the vortex. The negative pressure on the top of the wing and the positive pressure on the bottom of the wing meet each other at the wingtip and create this spiral or wingtip vortex. It can be very strong and wreak havoc on a trailing aircraft caught in its wake. The heavier the airplane, the stronger these little tornadoes. That is why the word *heavy* is used in their designation. These vortices have caused trailing airplanes to flip over and crash in the past.

Soon after this, the JAL "seven forty-seven heavy" takes off, and the tower calls to flight 587, "American five eight seven heavy, wind three zero zero at niner, runway three one left, cleared for takeoff."

First Officer Sten Molin then asks the captain, "You happy with that distance?" It's an important question. He's referring to the distance between their takeoff and the vortices left in the wake of the JAL.

"We'll be all right once we get rolling. He's supposed to be five miles by the time we're airborne. That's the idea." But the decision will be one of life or death for all aboard.

A few seconds later, at the 0913:47 time mark on the recorder, First Officer Molin reports, "Takeoff checks complete, I'm on the roll." Followed by the captain saying, "Thrust SRS, runway," and the sound of engines spooling up. "Eighty knots, thrust blue," he says.

Five seconds passes, and he calls, "V one."

One more second, "Rotate." Followed by, "V two plus ten."

Two seconds later, at 0914:30, First Officer Molin says, "Gear up, please." The plane is airborne.

At the 0914:47 mark, JFK control is heard, "American five eight seven heavy, turn left. Fly the Bridge Climb. Contact New York departure. Good morning." From this point, American five eight seven heavy will communicate with New York departure control instead of JFK tower.

By the 0915 mark, the Airbus has reached thirteen hundred feet, climbing to maintain five thousand.

"American five eight seven heavy, New York departure. Radar contact. Climb maintain one three thousand."

587 begins its left turn. Thirty-seven seconds later, there's the brief sound of a squeak and a rattle. A few seconds afterward, the captain says, "Little wake turbulence, huh?"

Molin, who has the controls, responds, "Yeah." Then the hot mic picks up a sound the report calls "five sets of stabilizer trim switch clicks," soon followed by the sound of a thump, a click, and two more thumps.

At the 0915:54 mark, First Officer Molin suddenly says, "Max power!" in a strained voice. This is their second encounter with the 747 wake turbulence. The captain asks Molin if he is all right, but he doesn't intervene or question the call for max power. Judging by the recording, both men are in agreement. But things escalate rapidly.

Within two seconds, the captain is saying, "Hang onto it. Hang onto it." His words are followed by the sound of a snap. According to the NTSB report, this is when the tail came off. In my mind, the specific time is questionable. We do know that at this time, Molin is all over the rudders, the ailerons, and the roll control. He tries everything to regain control. Again, he asks for full power. The CVR hears a loud thump and a bang and a roaring noise that increases. Then he swears and says, "What the hell are we into? We're stuck in it."

0916:14—the transmission ends.

At this time, the JAL 747 is ahead just a little over one nautical mile, almost one thousand feet above and off the right side of our Airbus. Calculations indicate that its wingtip vortex could still have about 80 percent of its potency and be right in the path of our Airbus.

Settlement

Flight 587 was a popular flight to the D.R. It was full of Dominican men commuting back from work in New Jersey and New York. At the time of the crash, my sailing ketch, *Caribana*, was moored in the harbor at Casa de Campo, La Romana, Dominican Republic. I had a good friend who had gone to the D.R. in the Peace Corps and stayed. We reconnected years later and did some diving on wrecks in the waters off Samaná Bay on the northeast end of Hispaniola. We also photographed whales calving on the Silver Banks. The connections that I had made over those years of sailing and diving in the D.R. resulted in several families seeking my help. I recall Johnnie Cochran being my biggest competition. We would stay in the same hotel while in Santo Domingo and trade courtroom lore.

The cases were assigned by the multidistrict panel to the federal court in Southern Manhattan.

From the beginning, it looked like all the cases would settle. But going to court, which I would have preferred, would have given me a chance to present the case before a judge and jury and to air an alternative view as to the probable cause of the crash as compared to that of the NTSB. I never did get that opportunity.

CHAPTER 13

TWA Airlines Flight 800

> *Pierre Salinger, JFK's speechwriter, was a significant voice in the prevalent noise and sinister conspiracy theory that* ***TWA 800*** *was shot down by a U.S. Navy missile*

Eyewitnesses saw a streak of light rising in the sky followed by a fireball. Some said the plane split in two as it descended toward the Atlantic Ocean off the southern coast of Suffolk County, Long Island. The captain of an eastward airliner reported to air traffic control, "I just saw an explosion out there," he said and then added, "It just went down into the water."

All souls including 18 crew and 212 passengers aboard the flight that night died. Early eyewitness reports led to speculation that TWA Flight 800 had been shot down by a surface-to-air missile or rocket.

This crash occurred in July of 1996, only three years after the 1993 World Trade Center bombing, so the idea of domestic terrorism was at least a possibility in people's minds. There was also an argument to be made that the large empty fuel tank in the center of the plane had exploded, a theory that, to investigators reviewing the wreckage, quickly became the most likely cause. You'll see why.

Legal Wrangling and the Investigation

I had several clients who had lost family and loved ones on Flight 800. The multidistrict litigation panel had assigned all cases, at least for discovery purposes, to the federal district court for the state of New York located in lower Manhattan. The court, over the objections of a couple New York firms, appointed me to the plaintiff's steering committee. A couple of much larger New York firms had been representing themselves as "the" aviation lawyers in the industry dating back to before I was in law school. In fact, they both had tried to hire me when I graduated. Now that I had come into my own, they had been putting up more and more resistance to my small boutique firm with offices in Colorado, Florida, and Michigan. I was playing in what they viewed as their sandbox.

The irony was that over the past several years, I had consulted with these same firms on aviation and technical issues. They would call and ask me about aeronautical engineering, piloting, or air traffic control procedures. I never charged for my help. At that time, I was a bit naive. I believed that we were members of the bar, and I should act with collegiality. They clearly didn't see things in the same light, especially when it came to an appointment to the plaintiff's steering committee

In the 1990s, the competition got fierce, and unscrupulous lawyers started to see gold in the air disaster business. Notwithstanding the competition, over the years, I continued to be appointed to the plaintiff's steering committee whenever I applied. I continued to believe that I could make airplanes safer in the courtroom.

During all the years that I have practiced, I attended simulator flight training at least twice a year, stayed current in at least two jets, and continued to fly many other general aviation airplanes. It was important to remain familiar with the environment of the air traffic control system and the instrument approaches to airports throughout the world. Additionally, it was necessary to stay current with mathematics, chemistry, physics, and materials science. In later years, maintaining an aerospace laboratory on the Rocky Mountain Metro Airport gave me the chance to employ scientists and engineers who kept me up-to-speed on the evolving state of the art and beyond.

The fact is, some of these air disasters did produce large legal fees. But for me, it was mostly an avocation. Largely, the fees became a way to fund more research, testing, and engineering analysis. For example, we purchased and instrumented several general aviation airplanes and a portion of a Boeing 737 to collect data and reconstruct accidents.

The investigation of TWA 800 was a monumental task. The team consisted of members of the NTSB, the FAA, some help from the military, and other government agencies. As usual, employees of Boeing and the engine and system's manufacturers were also part of the NTSB investigative team. The recovery of the remains of those onboard and the airplane parts took the better part of a year. Eventually, ninety-five percent of the aircraft was recovered and reassembled in an old Grumman hangar on Long Island. The work of the investigative teams was truly commendable. But as usual, Boeing had its brand to protect and the manufacturers of the aircraft systems knew that the passengers' survivors would have legal claims.

As usual, there were no engineers or reconstruction experts in the investigative process to protect the interests of the deceased. I felt an obligation to protect passengers from flaws that lay dormant in the operations, the airplane design, and maintenance. I suspected that there were several gremlins lurking in these jumbo jets. There were further legal issues such as, did the passengers experience pre-death terror or pain and suffering? Was there negligence on the part of the airline in the loading or flight planning? Was there negligence on the part of Boeing in the publishing of operating instructions? Were there product defects in the aircraft or its systems?

As part of the investigative style I had used since the earliest days of my practice, I always got out to the crash site and got my boots on the ground. There was no better way for me to understand what really happened.

In the case of TWA 800, this was difficult since the plane had broken up in-flight and fallen into the Atlantic Ocean miles offshore. My work was certainly cut out for me. I wanted to learn everything possible about how and why 230 people lost their lives in Boeing's first jumbo jet. The B 747-100 series was now more than twenty-five years old.

Sometime after the accident recovery effort and reassembly of the Boeing 747, I flew out to Long Island and landed at KFOK airport, which served West Hampton. It was after dark on a Sunday night.

There wasn't much that I could do that night, so I rented a car and headed out toward Montauk to find a place to spend the night and contemplate a plan. As I lay in bed that night, I was thinking about how the jumbo jet in its initial climb out of JFK had exploded more than two miles above the Atlantic and left a debris field about three and a half miles long and a mile wide in the ocean.

Ever since my trip to South America in the 1938 Lockheed Electra, scuba diving had been a part of my life, and I decided that night that since the sea was forecasted to be less than two-foot waves and light wind the next day, I should get out on the ocean and view the site from a perspective that I would never really feel from reading the accident reports. When checking the soundings on the maritime charts, I further noted that the depth in the area where the debris had rained down was roughly between 100 and 150 feet. To me, that was in the neighborhood of comfortable diving.

The next morning, I left the harbor at Montauk in a 23-feet rigid-hull inflatable boat, (known as a RIB Boat). I had a couple of tanks with 3,000 psi air, a wet suit, and my dive gear. About four and a half miles out, I stopped and gazed up, trying to imagine the big jet with the forward part of the fuselage blown off and over 200 passengers maybe looking through a rim of fire into the night sky. (Yet the reality is, after the blast of the explosion and the resulting shock wave, I doubted that anyone was alive.) The data showed that most of the passenger section, without the crew, climbed another 3,000 feet, up to about 16,000 feet, before plunging into the ocean.

Next, I donned the dive gear, tied a line around my waist with a slip bowline, and made a slow descent. I found the bottom just below 100 feet. It was murky and limited visibility. I drifted for a while. I didn't find a whole lot. But the recovery process was integral to understanding the wreckage as a whole. It was important to see the conditions under which the plane had been salvaged and what the bottom looked like, etc. But more than anything, it was my normal M.O. aside from any stated goal to get as close to every crash site as possible.

Diving the deep-blue water where 230 men and women had perished was sobering. These were the stakes of air travel the way it seemed to be evolving. You could feel the weight of their deaths with a hundred feet of water over you. Out in the Atlantic, it became more than clear not only that we needed to fully understand what caused the plane to explode (without the phantom pressure from insurance companies and the typical slant to blame pilot error), but also to try to prevent it from happening again.

The close sense of human loss is also something you can't get from reading a report, crunching numbers, or watching a computer-generated crash re-enactment. It is hard to say what you would gain from such a visit before going. It could be as simple as an observation that turns the key to understanding why the plane came down, or it could be very little indeed; it's never nothing.

With Flight 800, what did I find?

I didn't find wreckage or a poorly-designed fuel selector valve like in the Beechcraft case, but I saw the same sky through which the B747 was making its departure climb headed for Paris, the sky in which it exploded, and the ocean floor where the pieces ultimately came to rest.

Geographically, where the pieces and the passengers entered the surface of the ocean was ultimately of great legal importance.

The defense lawyers were arguing that the territorial waters of the United States went out only three miles from shore. It was their argument that the TWA flight had crashed into the sea outside of U.S. territorial waters and was thus controlled by the "Death on the High Seas Act" rather than by the laws of the state of New York. The wrongful death law of New York provided for substantially better compensation, an example of some of the legal wrangling that, though often boring, greatly impacts victims. On this issue, we prevailed after finding an executive order of President Reagan extending the territorial waters of New York out to twelve miles.

I emphasized the concept of physically visiting the crash site because boots on the ground has never been the fashion among trial lawyers, and it's almost non-existent now. This trend of remaining locked behind a keyboard currently crosses all boundaries of life.

Today when we hire private detectives, they for the most part do their work online. It's hard to find a real super-sleuth anymore.

Likewise, I find that young engineers more and more believe that running a flight simulation on a computer is the same as physical flight testing and collecting empirical data. It is not. There is most often something missing when one tries to digitally simulate reality.

Consistent with this concept, I had learned from keeping my ear to the wall that the team had substantially reassembled the wrecked B747, piece-by-piece, in an old Grumman hangar at Calverton on Long Island. My plane was at the airport near Westhampton. I had returned to Montauk after spending the day on the ocean east of Long Island. That night, I got a map of the island and located the town of Calverton. I decided that in the morning it might be a good idea to get my bike from the plane and ride over to Calverton and do a little snooping around.

The next day, I put on some old jeans and a ratty pair of old tennis shoes and rode up to the old Grumman hangar. I figured that if I showed up in a suit and tie at the front door looking like a lawyer, I would be turned away immediately. When I got to the hangar, it was starting to rain quite heavily. I saw several cars parked in the front, some with U.S. government license plates. I decided to ride around to the back. Just as I rounded the building, I saw someone partially open a small man door. The rain was perfect cover. I yelled, "Can you hold the door a minute?" He seemed glad to help me get out of the rain. I don't know where that man went, but I never saw him again. Nevertheless, there I was inside. I'm not sure that getting in would be so easy today.

I would have been in trouble if discovered and likely brought before the judge in lower Manhattan. If nothing else, I would have been scolded, maybe kicked off the plaintiff's steering committee, or held in contempt. I had been there before. The New York lawyers, who were my competitors, would likely have been gleeful. However, getting caught wasn't in the cards.

Notwithstanding the apparent risk, I felt justified. We know that the manufacturers had been here, and I'm sure that their insurance companies had been briefed and likely had pictures.

I grabbed a broom and tried to look like I belonged. What I saw was very impressive. The NTSB and its contractors had done a great job of reconstructing the airplane. It is hard to imagine the B747, which had exploded two miles above the Atlantic Ocean, could be salvaged and reassembled piece-by-piece and be recognized as an airliner. The NTSB had reconstructed the airplane from the pieces divers and scallop trollers had retrieved from the bottom of the ocean. They had found almost about 95 percent of the plane. Inside the fuselage, you could even see the passenger seats in their original locations. The entire reproduction was held together by a kind of papier-mâché with mesh and wire.

What the reconstruction showed clearly was that the center wing tank had exploded from within. It was obvious that this airplane had not been brought down by a missile or a rocket. From my view, we didn't need to look any further. However, theories about Flight 800 having been shot down by the National Guard or the Navy had gained some traction in the news media.

Some months later, and as I recall after the issuance of the NTSB report, during the legal discovery process, the New York Federal District Court granted a motion that permitted the lawyers on the plaintiff's steering committee to visit the reconstructed B747 at the Grumman hangar. This was a court-sanctioned official viewing and somewhat limited.

During the protracted period of investigation and under the control of the NTSB, the conspiracy theories went on.

The Master of Disaster

The twenty-four-hour news cycle is fed by catastrophe and drama. That there was interest in this angle wasn't unusual, but too many of us on the committee knew the driving force behind this bogus conspiracy theory. I believed that it was greater than a mere conspiracy theory. Specifically, we thought Boeing was maintaining the story's prominence and giving it legs. Not exactly to shift blame but to obfuscate, to muddy the water, and to dispel the thought in the public's collective view that anything could be wrong with the B747 or with its fuel system.

I realize that claiming Boeing, or its council, would seize upon and magnify the possibility of the shot-down theory being proliferated in the media might seem strange at first, but it's much less strange when one considers what the goal of such a narrative would be. Namely, to defend the brand itself. If a large portion of the population thinks the plane might have been downed by terrorists or by our own government, then there's no reason to fear the design and no reason to doubt the brand, which in this case was Boeing. The effort represents a public relations campaign to cause people to conclude anything but the real cause. The real cause being an empty center-wing fuel tank, a problem that is potentially a problem with several large transport airplanes and especially with the Boeing 747, as history shows.

The PR effort appeared to have the hallmarks of someone whom we had come to know, the "Master of Disaster." He was a partner in a major law firm with close ties to Boeing and its insurers going back decades. Both Boeing and the insurance companies counted on him to do his magic in disasters such as this. He was a fierce man, prone, or rather, skilled in non-traditional and guerrilla defense tactics. I might not have liked him, but I had to respect his ability and boldness.

I remember a previous instance with this man. We had sued Boeing in a case where a small corporate jet in trail behind a Boeing 757 was flipped over while on final approach to KBIL, serving Billings, Montana. The crash was fatal. The Boeing 757 had a reputation of shedding a strong and lethal wingtip vortex. The vorticity of this airplane was the worst in the industry, yet Boeing consistently denied there was any safety issue in the face of a plethora of documentation to the contrary. It was the opinion of leading experts on aerodynamics that it was the configuration of the wing flaps that was the culprit.

In the case in question, involving the "Master of Disaster," somewhere in my reconnaissance, I had come across an internal Boeing memo wherein the company essentially admitted that the 757 vortices were, in fact, a greater danger to trailing aircraft than most others, even including the heavy larger airplanes, which necessarily have greater lift. While I was taking the deposition of a Boeing engineer in Boeing's counsel's office in Seattle regarding the Montana case, during cross-examination, I reached into my case and took out a copy of the Boeing internal memo pertaining to the 757 vortex issue. I handed it to the court reporter and asked that it be marked as an exhibit for identification. Boeing's lawyer had no idea that I had this "smoking gun" internal memo or how I got it. The "Master of Disaster" stood up abruptly, looked at the exhibit, and grabbed it. He put it in his case and said quite loudly that, "This deposition is over." He then left the deposition room with the memo.

He must have thought that he took the only copy. "Keep it for your records," I said as he left. "I have the original."

At that point, I got up and left. I went down to the street level. The street ran along the waterfront on Puget Sound. I walked for about a block and found the classical raw bar. I went in, sat at the bar, and ordered some lunch. While having some tasty oysters, I thought, he could be found in contempt for his behavior at a court-sanctioned deposition, and possibly for destruction of evidence. His actions were a little crazy. As I pondered my options, all of the sudden, someone sat down beside me. It was the "Master of Disaster."

"We have to talk," he said. He wanted to settle the case.

This story goes to show how far an aggressive advocate might go for his client. The subtlety of a red-herring public relations campaign (the shot-down stories) to distract attention from this horrific event, to save the representation of the Boeing brand, would have been less likely to incur blowback compared to other stunts I was familiar with.

Was there really such a campaign to distract from the fuel tank explosion? I don't have in my possession a memo that proves it. But at the time, we knew that there was a paid counternarrative.

Pierre Salinger began writing articles and giving speeches pushing the theory that the U.S. Navy had shot the plane down. Pierre was no dark horse. He had been the press secretary to President John F. Kennedy and later worked in corporate public relations, until becoming the Paris Bureau Chief for ABC News. By 1993, he was working as a consultant for the public relations firm Burson-Marsteller.

I don't have a window inside his thinking, but from our perspective at the time, not only in our firm but others, we viewed his campaign in favor of the shot-down theory as a public relations move—a tactic to divert public attention from reality. In hindsight, he certainly was the right man for the job.

Boeing had a brand to protect after all—the 747 was its marquee. Boeing's insurance company also had a lot of money at stake. Both were highly interested in what would be stated as the probable cause of the crash of TWA Flight 800. There was a clear motive to deflect attention in the public eye away from a Boeing jumbo jet being blown out of the sky because of a product defect.

If people believed that a 747 had been taken down by a missile, that was one thing, but a fuel tank explosion is the type of accident that can happen again. It may not happen often. However, it has some history that can't be ignored.

Flying Fuel-Air Bomb

The military had for years been concerned about the potential dangers of empty fuel tanks having an explosive mixture of air and fuel under certain conditions. Boeing had built the KC-135 tankers for the military. After midair refueling of a large bomber like the B52 (also a Boeing aircraft), the tanker would be returning to base with large empty fuel tanks. All aircraft have a certain amount of unusable fuel because of the structural design. Under certain conditions of pressure and temperature, the atmosphere in the tank above the unusable fuel, known as ullage, can become a very combustible mixture of fuel, vapor, and air. This mixture being contained in a closed volume, such as a large fuel tank, can be highly explosive. Basically, the airplane can become a flying fuel-air bomb. All that is required is enough heat to reach the fuel's flash point and ignition.

The fueling tankers, like the KC-135, fly at high altitudes where the temperature is quite low, like −40 degrees Celsius, (−40 Celsius is also −40 Fahrenheit), well-below the flash point of military-grade jet fuel, the temperature above which fuel vapor will ignite. Interesting to our story, the military uses fuel that has a considerably higher flash point than Jet A fuel used by commercial airliners. It's on this point where the story of how TWA Flight 800 came down begins.

In most conditions under which commercial airplanes operate, the fuel never warms above its flash point, which for our purposes is about 100 degrees Fahrenheit for Jet A. The trouble is that fuel in commercial jets doesn't always stay below 100 degrees. Rising above that point doesn't mean there will be a fire, but it is the first step in creating the conditions necessary for one. In the case of TWA Flight 800, the plane had been delayed on the ground at JFK Airport for more than an hour due to a piece of disabled ground equipment and some confusion over passenger luggage. The temperature taken at JFK that day was 80 degrees. The temperature on the tarmac would likely be hotter. Although close, the temperature on the ground would not have been sufficient to heat the fuel tanks beyond the flash point. But there is another factor to consider.

As TWA Flight 800 sat on the tarmac for an extended period of time, the captain kept the air-conditioning packs running in order to keep the passengers comfortable. There was nothing in the operating limitations prohibiting this; in fact, it was standard procedure. But one of the air-conditioning packs is located directly below the center-wing tank, which was essentially empty except for the unusable fuel since the flight to Charles De Gaulle Airport in France didn't require a full fuel load and weight is always a performance issue.

The unusable fuel in the essentially empty center-wing tank would be close to one hundred gallons. This was clearly enough to fill the atmosphere in this large tank with fuel vapor. When full, this tank holds several thousand gallons of fuel.

In tests conducted after the crash, the NTSB determined that the surface of the pertinent air-conditioning pack reached over 200 degrees, and the temperature of the center-wing fuel tank reached 123 degrees on the runway and had fallen to 117 degrees by the time the plane reached 14,000 feet, the altitude at which it exploded. In other words, the conditions in the center-wing fuel tank were ripe for ignition.

There is precedent for exploding fuel tanks on aircraft. One most memorable to me was a case in which I represented the plaintiff in state court in Jacksonville, Florida. The aircraft was a light twin-engine Beechcraft known as a Travel Air. The plane had been in for some maintenance, after which it had been tied down outside for several days. The owner picked it up late one afternoon after it had been sitting out on the tarmac in the Florida sun. After settling up the bill with the maintenance company, the owner taxied out for takeoff. He had skipped adding fuel since the plane had a little less than half fuel, which was plenty for his intended hop over to Gainesville. Having been cleared onto the departure runway, he advanced the throttles and began his takeoff roll. Just before his rotational speed there was a giant explosion. The airplane and everything in the vicinity were obliterated by the explosion, including a piece of the runway. The only thing that was immediately recognizable of the pilot was a piece of his underwear. The maintenance records showed that a red navigation light on the left wing had been repaired, including its wiring, which ran through the left wing. A section of the wing structure was also the left fuel tank. The case was against the maintenance company.

In the case of TWA 800, the exact cause of the ignition was never clearly proven, either by the plaintiff's steering committee or the NTSB. Many wanted to press the idea that some kind of an electric short had caused it, as in the Jacksonville case. However, my argument was that the fuel vapor itself didn't require an electric spark for ignition. Static electricity would have been enough to set it off, once the explosive condition was met. The problem, as I saw it, centered on flying planes with an empty fuel tank and the presence of fuel vapor at or near the flash point. While in terms of probability the chance of explosion is small, but explosion is possible once the conditions are met. They are likely met every day somewhere in the world.

Often, I disagree with positions taken by the NTSB. However, in this case, I did agree with the Board in its "Executive Summary" where the Board stated, "Contributing factors to the accident were the design certification concept that fuel tank explosions could be prevented solely by precluding all ignition sources and design and certification of the Boeing 747 with heat sources located beneath the CWT with no means to reduce the heat transferred into the CWT or to render the fuel vapor in the tank nonflammable." The sentence is a real mouthful, not to mention convoluted, but in short, removing ignition sources from the fuel tanks isn't enough to prevent an explosion. The air/fuel mixture might ignite anyway. Likewise, heating the empty tanks (and any fuel remaining) to a temperature above the flash point by proximity to air-conditioning units is a bad idea that creates the conditions for an explosion.

It has been suggested for many years that large empty fuel tanks could be protected from air/fuel vapor by replacing the air with an inert gas. That is, a gas that would not undergo a chemical reaction under the circumstances. Since it is the oxygen in the air that supports combustion, it makes sense to take the air out of the equation. Bottled nitrogen is an example of such a solution.

In 1998, before the NTSB's final report on the TWA crash, the Aviation Rulemaking Advisory Committee (ARAC) convened a fuel tank working group at the behest of the FAA. This group was known as the "FUEL TANK HARMONIZATION WORKING GROUP," and its report concluded that center-tank explosions were a problem. It noted that all the crashes and explosions involved Jet A and A1 fuels.

It went on to state, "These tanks have not yet reached the safety level attained by wing tanks, and that action to further reduce the flammability levels in center tanks should be considered." Flammability levels here referred to the amount of oxygen in the atmosphere of the empty tank. Again, no O_2, no fire.

The study also "identified and analyzed 16 known instances of fuel tank explosions [other than those following impacts with the ground] over the past 40 years." According to their number, the center-wing fuel tank of transport aircraft operations explode worldwide on average every two and a half years. A fact that I never would have guessed. If the center tank on TWA 800 exploded, it represents a design defect that must be corrected. It also goes a long way to explain why pushing the idea of a rocket attack on the plane was better than having the truth largely believed.

In 2001, this working group released a second report, which recommended no rulemaking action but suggested more research. This seems like a stall tactic due to the projected cost of inerting the tanks. Finally, on July 21, 2008, the FAA published a final rule on the reduction of fuel tank flammability in transport category airplanes with a new requirement to "mitigate the effects of flammability tank vapors" to acceptable levels by mandating the installation of either a flammability reduction means (FRM) or ignition mitigation means.

This a step in the right direction, however, very late in coming. And what does it mean to existing aircraft and/or those added to type certificates that were issued fifty years ago?

I do believe that what we did in this case rekindled the effort to eliminate the risk of letting air transports being bombs waiting to explode.

CHAPTER 14

Tail Power and the Boeing 737

*Only fools and dead men don't change
their minds. Fools won't. Dead men can't.*

—*John H. Patterson*

A Boeing 737 went down just outside Colorado Springs in March of 1991. At a thousand feet above ground, on approach, the plane rolled steeply right and continued rolling until it flew nearly vertical into the ground. The impact was catastrophic and left a fifteen-foot crater of debris and remains.

It was a Sunday morning and I was in our law office at Jeffco Airport, which later became Rocky Mountain Metro Airport, just north of Denver. One of our pilots called my cell phone within fifteen minutes of the crash. He remembered that I had often critiqued the 737 in the past and said that I was his first call.

In truth, I had thought a lot about the 737 those years after I had left Boeing. For one thing, I always thought that hanging the fan-jet engines so far out on the wing was a bad idea. It was an issue of weight, vulnerability to foreign object ingestion, and asymmetric thrust. As I mentioned in my previous chapter on Boeing, because of this geometry, it was necessary to use a massive vertical stabilizer and rudder to counter the asymmetric thrust of the operating engine with one engine inoperative. The distance of these engines out from the centerline would cause several crashes and the loss of many lives, including those lost in the Colorado Springs crash.

In turn, the large vertical stabilizer and rudder give the airplane too much tail power. That is, the power to yaw the airplane and to swing the nose left and right. With an excessive amount of tail power, in a swept-wing airplane, it's easy to get too much roll-yaw coupling. The result can be more roll with the rudder than with the ailerons, which are the intended roll-control devices. In the event of an errant rudder hard-over with too much tail power, the airplane can roll uncontrollably.

Additionally, the engines were too close to the ground and were like big vacuum cleaners that picked up debris, causing foreign object damage known as FOD. Also, fan-jet engines were growing in diameter because fan bypass ratio was predicted to grow since more fan bypass was more efficient. Fan bypass ratio refers to the amount of air that enters the engine inlet and bypasses the core of the turbo jet and exits out the rear. The subject of engine bypass will take center stage in the next chapter on the Boeing 737 MAX, a plane that is also an add-on to the original 737 type certificate. On the Max, the bypass was so great that it was necessary to shift the engine location to accommodate the greater diameter. The result would become a stability and control problem.

When I was a young engineer in flight test at Boeing, I was actively aware of Boeing's goal to come up with a short-haul jet airliner, which they believed was the best approach to remaining competitive. The three-engine Boeing 727 was the first answer. Technically it was a well-thought-out airplane. The design was led by the engineering department, while business management, economists, and marketing didn't seem to be meddling in the engineering details. Unfortunately, the 727 wasn't a great economic success. Boeing needed something to compete with the DC-9 along with a few European manufacturers. By now they were already late to a growing small airliner market, which was becoming dominated with more economical airplanes.

The concept of the two-engine airplane that would ultimately become the 737 was discussed in preliminary design meetings just as the 727 was getting certified. However, the actual 737 program wasn't officially announced until 1964, as a twin-engine, small airliner carrying eighty-five passengers and positioned to fight for market share against the Caravelle, the BAC-111, and the DC-9.

While I had left Boeing before the 737 was certified, they kept the basic design, which I had originally criticized. My complaint regarding engine placement still stood and does to this day. But the response to my complaint as a young engineer had come from the marketing department. They said, "We are Boeing, and Boeing airplanes have their engines on the wings." Furthermore, "If we put the engines in closer to the airplane centerline on the rear of the fuselage, it will look like a DC-9."

This response was among the factors that led me to leave the company. In a way, the 737 concept made my career. It marked the moment I realized I couldn't effect change as a young engineer in the aircraft industry. I thought, there must be a better way.

I had also suggested that if we were going to end up with a very large vertical tail, we should at least split the rudder into two panels to mitigate the effect of an errant rudder hard-over, which I was concerned about because high-pressure hydraulic control systems can be unpredictable. We had split the rudder on the 727 for such a reason. But it wasn't done on the 737. I suspect it was an economic issue.

A Personal Investigation

While my new work took me away from Boeing, I never forgot the design experience while there. So, when I learned about the fatal roll at Colorado Springs, I was curious and wanted to know why.

I decided to dig into the crash on my own.

My personal office was only about eighty miles from Colorado Springs. At the time, we were a rather small firm, though we did have other offices on the airport in Fort Lauderdale, Florida, and in Detroit, Michigan. Our Colorado office is where we were instrumenting and testing airplanes to reconstruct accidents or create demonstrative evidence for use in the courtroom. There, we had a good shop and had designed some special transducers, sensors, and recording devices.

Doing so had given us more technical freedom, flexibility, and agility than our competitor law firms. This flexibility included taking deep dives into design problems. In this case, the manner in which the 737 had gone out of control and crashed at Colorado Springs really piqued my interest.

In other words, it had the characteristics of rolling out of control consistent with swept-wing roll-yaw coupling, resulting from an unintended full-rudder deflection. The basic facts gave reason to think about what excess tail power could do in swept-wing airplanes.

As reports of the crash stated, it was windy that Sunday morning, March 1, 1991. United Airlines Flight 585 had just lined up for final approach to runway 35 at the Colorado Springs airport. Witnesses say the 737 rolled to the right and then pitched down into Widefield Park, a narrow long park filled with playground equipment. One witness, Larry Abegglen, told the *Washington Post* that he was watching television when he "looked out the living room window and saw the plane roll over on its right side and go into the ground." Normally, the park would have been filled with children, but thankfully, it was a blustery cool Sunday morning and empty.

Everyone onboard including two flight crew, three flight attendants, and twenty passengers were killed. The conditions of the remains were more awful than one can imagine. Backhoes were needed to remove the unidentifiable remains from the crater. Although the loss of life in terms of numbers was small compared to some of the other air disasters, it seemed that Boeing was disproportionately protective about what this crash said about their best-selling workhorse. We further noted strange stories as to the cause of this crash floated in the press. For one thing, I received a strange phone call some months after the crash. The anonymous caller said that I might want to know about the romantic affair that existed between the male captain and the female co-pilot of this United Airlines flight.

The caller said it might tell me why the plane crashed. He then hung up. This was the first I'd heard of the story, but as I began to represent deceased passengers' families and loved ones, the story about the flight crew kept coming up.

I wasn't the only one who was hearing it either. Clients were telling me that Boeing was spreading a rumor. The story was now going around that the captain, a fifty-one-year-old married man with a child, was having an affair with the co-pilot, forty-two-year-old woman. As the story went, the co-pilot broke the news that she wanted to call things off just before the landing. Impeccable timing. Her decision enraged the pilot, who then grabbed the cockpit fire axe, buried it into her head, and then crashed the plane. The story didn't mention the details as to how the pilot flew the plane into the ground.

The captain's widow told a *Westword* reporter that the story was created by the airline industry. As she said, "They [Boeing officials] don't want to say they were wrong. They wanted to push it off on someone else. They don't want to be responsible." Taking everything into consideration, it looked that way to me also. The axe rumor never made it to the local papers. It was however mentioned in a *Newsday* article in New York and in a second paper in Florida. Supposedly, the cockpit fire axe had been found and was covered in blood and brain tissue, suggesting that the information was leaked from the official investigation.

As an attorney on the plaintiff's steering committee, I had to deal with the axe murder story. It would have been malpractice to just let it linger. I therefore had a subpoena with a "duces tecum" (to bring stuff) prepared and served on the coroner of El Paso County. He had control of the human remains and the body bags. The lawyers and respective experts then appeared at the coroner's facility and examined the remains.

Although there were the same number of bags as passengers and crew, the pathology was all mixed up. Individuals were eventually identified by dental records and other methods. The whole event was a horrible experience.

After two days of examining the remains and consulting with our pathology experts, it was concluded that the axe story was donkey dust.

We had no idea where the story came from or any means of tracing it. Was it just another outrageous diversionary trick? If the story had gotten legs, or if the co-pilot's body had been discovered with a gash in the head, we would be doing a whole different case, but again, these stunts were never about the facts. It was really about muddying the waters and playing with the hearts and minds of people, hoping to have some effect on the public's perception and maybe the NTSB's conclusion. Today it would have been in social media without any accountability and maybe develop a life of its own and "go viral." My sense is that this giant of the industry needed to deflect any thought that the 737, its most profitable item, suffered from a basic design defect, as the idea that it was a dangerous airplane would be an uncontrollable cancer to the manufacturer.

A Little Luck and the National Center for Atmospheric Research

I was increasingly leaning in the direction that the Colorado Springs crash was caused by the large rudder on the oversized vertical stabilizer doing something other than what the pilot commanded it to do. The unintended maneuver was a classic aerodynamic fit for a machine with this geometry. What I didn't know yet is what the rudder did to get so out of phase with the intended input. However, I did know that it was an all-hydraulic system. I also knew that hydraulic valving under high pressure can do some crazy, unpredictable things. But without having actually looked into the matter and conducting some tests, I couldn't be sure. It was a hunch, but a well-informed one and a good starting point.

I was also busy thinking about how Boeing would defend a claim for a defective design as I was drafting a complaint to file in the federal district court in Colorado.

Then I got lucky, or fate intervened, on my behalf.

On Tuesday nights, I used to play golf in a men's league at the Boulder Country Club, which I had done for years. This night, my partner, Brad Griffin, who had survived the United Airlines Flight 232 crash in Sioux City, and I had been paired against a team of two other players whom we had never met. Brad and I had been friends ever since the case where I represented him. He still putted with the bent putter found in the wreckage.

In the course of the match, one of our opponents mentioned that he worked at the National Center for Atmospheric Research (NCAR).

When I heard that, I said, "Oh, so you work for the government."

"No, NCAR's a private company, but we do a lot of work for the government. Right now, I am working for Boeing. They want us to try and find, or create, a rotor meteorological condition that can roll over a Boeing 737 like what happened at Colorado Springs when United Airlines crashed."

"Wow," I said. "That's pretty interesting."

I would later learn that NCAR had been formally hired by the NTSB. It's referenced in their 1992 report. But regardless of how the NTSB spins the job they gave NCAR, this young man I was playing golf with understood that he and his co-workers were asked to create some evidence to explain why the 737 went out of control other than the roll-yaw coupling driven by the power of the very large vertical stabilizer and large rudder that had gone awry.

I had now learned at least one of the defenses that I might face at trial, and by this time, I had developed some good expert witnesses on meteorology, so I put them on the wind rotor issue.

The wind rotor defense is typically referred to as an "Act of God," a favorite defense for manufacturers since God has no insurance and doesn't accept subpoenas. Regardless of whether it was a plausible cause for the crash or not, I had to be well-prepared to cross-examine their NCAR meteorologist. An interesting quip: many meteorologists were TV weathermen early in their careers, and so one of my first questions on cross-examination always was, "You were a TV weatherman, weren't you?"

No one believes a TV weatherman.

Judging from the cockpit voice recorder (CVR), something sudden and drastic happened to that airplane. But what was it? I knew that I had to listen to the tape myself. I wanted to hear what the crew said in those final moments. Also, I wanted to do my own sound spectrum analysis. In addition to the voices, the CVR also picks up a lot of sounds. We had the ability to determine the frequency of the various sounds, and from this, we might find out what buttons were pushed, what levers were moved, what pumps were running, and maybe the condition of the engines.

The CVR tape was in the hands of the NTSB. They would only give up a copy, but I wanted the original since sounds might be filtered or otherwise lost in the copying process. After a motion to produce and extensive argument in court by the lawyers representing the Department of Justice, we were given the tape for a couple of days with many restrictions and government security present the entire time we had access.

The tape indicated that the approach was going according to plan that windy morning and that the engines were running equally as they should for this mode of flight. The flight data recorder (FDR) indicated that the plane had just begun its descent on the glideslope when all of the sudden, the airplane rolled steeply to the right. According to the tape, the crew was struggling to right the plane, and they were screaming. They went down in a matter of seconds; there was little time to think. Additionally, there was no indication of any issues between the captain and the first officer.

To me, the 737's massive vertical stabilizer and proportionally large rudder were the obvious culprits. No pilot would be able counter the roll caused by a rudder hard-over or blow-down at this approach speed and configuration (i.e., wing flaps extended). This loss of control was a distinct possibility ever since this airplane was laid out on the drawing board all those years ago. The NTSB explains the trouble well in the updated version of its 2002 report.

As they put it, "The rudders on airplanes with fuselage-mounted engines are typically less powerful than the rudders on airplanes with wing-mounted engines." They further explain why. The Board explained a concept that I had complained about since the 1960s: "The rudders for fuselage-mounted engine airplanes do not have to be designed to counter a significant asymmetrical thrust effect in the event of a loss of power on one engine." I might have said it better myself, but the NTSB was accurate. The same footnote argues that "because the rudder on airplanes with the fuselage-mounted engines is less powerful, the consequences of a rudder hard-over are less serious."

Very much less serious, and that's the point.

Put another way: because the rudder on airplanes with wing-mounted engines is MORE powerful, the consequences of a rudder hard-over can be catastrophic. Although buried in a footnote, this is the heart of the matter for this crash. But what caused Flight 585's rudder hard-over? For the purposes of collecting money damages for my clients, I'm not sure that knowing the specific mechanism causing the errant rudder was necessary, but I wanted to understand the details! I didn't want to see this happen again and it seemed obvious that a latent design defect wouldn't happen only once. But, I could never have predicted how soon or how often it would happen again.

My interest was piqued again when Copa Airlines Flight 201 crashed not long after takeoff from Panama City, killing forty-seven people. It was June 1992, and the way that the plane went down was eerily similar to United 585. Again, early speculation said it was a rudder problem. But as usual, there was a lot of speculation as to other causes, such as the attitude indicator, wind shear, and a few others.

In subsequent 737 crashes and incidents caused by design problems, there's always a crazy story floated to divert the fault from the airplane design. It seems like Boeing will regularly create an alternative cause that will end up in the media or even in the NTSB report. Even today with the fatal crashes of the 737 MAX, I'm starting to hear some outrageous alternative causes floating around.

Just before the Copa Airlines crash at Panama City, top Boeing officials held a secret meeting because of their concern about the rudder's hydraulic servo-control valve and the fact that the 737 was the only airliner of its time with two engines out on the wing and a single rudder panel. They ultimately decided that since the rudder problem was more of an irritating maintenance problem than a life-or-death issue, and as the crashes were a mere trifle compared to the number of 737s in service, the matter was tabled.

Lawyers from Panama City called my office, asking for some help. We had several conversations, and I shared what I could. We went over the tail power issue and the inability of the ailerons to counter a roll caused by a rudder hard-over. I discussed my concerns with the hydraulic servo units and the possibility of high-pressure valves to mis-port and/or jam.

In this instance, the NTSB in its final report set aside the errant rudder as a cause. They hung their hat on a series of alternative theories.

I had my doubts as to the correctness of their "probable cause."

There was little I could do with these doubts. However, in November of that year, another 737 crashed as the crew tried to land at Guilin Qifengling Airport in Guangxi, China. This China Southern Airlines Flight 3943 disaster killed 141 people. I was not an attorney for any of the families then, but I studied the facts in detail because it had the classic signature of another un-commanded rudder movement.

The aircraft had an auto-throttle system, which operated the power levers to maintain a selected airspeed. One of the levers failed to advance when it should have. The result was a substantial asymmetric thrust that called for substantial rudder input, and the rudder seemed to go to the blowdown position in the direction opposite of what the pilot selected.

After these two additional crashes, the NTSB came out with its report on the Colorado Springs crash. This was December of 1992. Their findings would seal my determination to get to the bottom of things. The opening line read, "This report documents the inexplicable loss of United Flight 585."

Inexplicable? I assumed the inexplicable was that they couldn't find a meteorological rotor that could bring the plane down, and they weren't willing to blame Boeing.

Experiments with the Empennage of a Boeing 737

I was even more motivated now. The idea that a plane could crash in Colorado Springs in the 1990s and we couldn't explain why sounded silly. I had had enough of these games. The Springs crash happened to be one of only four airline crashes that the NTSB hadn't come to a resolution on, which is significant.

The focus of the report was on two areas: "a malfunction of the airplane's lateral or directional control system or an encounter with an unusually severe atmospheric disturbance."

But the reason to rule out an atmospheric disturbance was latent in the NTSB report, which cited several meteorological events responsible for airplane accidents in the past, but all of them, including the B52 bomber over Spanish Peak, had suffered a structural failure as a result of their weather encounter. They hadn't simply rolled over and flown into the ground; they were broken first.

My first task was to read every training manual and technical report until I knew the 737 rudder system from the foot pedals to the rudder itself. I had a good understanding of the stability and control and the aerodynamics of the airplane. I needed to get a better understanding of the rudder control mechanism, including the power control unit and servo valve, because I wanted to understand the various possible failure modes.

To do so, I needed to acquire an actual B737 empennage and its entire hardware assembly. It didn't take long. First, I found a complete rudder power control unit (PCU) for sale in Peru of all places. I purchased that unit and brought it back to our facility in Broomfield, Colorado. We then purchased a complete 737 tail section from an airplane boneyard in Tucson and had it shipped to our hangar.

I worked with Don Sommer and a few other pilots and potential expert witnesses to create our little simulator. When mounted on the airplane, the vertical stabilizer was thirty-seven feet tall. We designed a low dolly and were able to mount our tail to reach only about twenty feet off the hangar floor. We had done some reverse engineering and were able to fully rig the vertical stabilizer, the rudder, the trim feel system, the power control unit with the servo valve, and a set of rudder pedals, as they would have been in an actual plane. We even put a pilot's seat on the dolly from where we could sit to operate the rudders and also had the plane painted in the same colors as one of the planes that went down. I thought it should look the part. By this point, we were ready to do some experiments and collect empirical data.

Some years prior, I had developed a great respect for the potential faults and shortcomings of high-pressure hydraulic systems, especially those using shuttle valves to port fluid to accomplish various tasks. The 737 rudder servo valve was such an animal. I had made the discovery when I tried a series of product liability cases involving Ford hydraulic automatic transmissions, models C4, C6, and FMS. When selecting Park on the shifting display known as the "PRNDL," the shuttle valves with certain tolerance stack-ups would mis-port, sending the fluid to command reverse. There were some horrible accidents where children behind the cars were run over and injured or killed.

In those days, it wasn't clear how these unintended modes were happening, and Ford didn't have a meteorological rotor to blame. To figure it out, I had purchased a transmission of each model and started experimenting in my garage in Lake Orion, Michigan. With some tinkering, I found the trouble lay not in the basic design but in the tolerance stack-up of the shuttle valve parts. Specifically, I found that if I had the maximum ID (inside diameter) on the valve body and minimum OD (outside diameter) on the slide or shuttle, then the hydraulic fluid could leak to an unintended port, such as from park to reverse.

In our little 737 rudder simulator, I was able to duplicate the same type of mis-porting due to tolerances. I could also cause a mis-porting if the secondary slide would jam because of tolerances or debris. Interestingly, most of the instances where we duplicated mis-porting, there were no telltale marks on the hardware, which at the time many people didn't think was possible. But the empirical data (i.e., the evidence) was right in our hangar for anyone to see.

While I was able to use our tail mock-up to settle some of our 585 cases, the industry wasn't listening.

Would it take another horrible crash? The very sad truth is, it did! It wouldn't take long.

USAir Flight 427

It was September 1994, USAir Flight 427 from Chicago's O'Hare to Pittsburgh crashed, killing the two pilots, three flight attendants, and all 127 passengers. This time, the NTSB finally caved to the pressure and blamed the problematic rudder. In its summary, the Board stated, "The National Transportation Safety Board determines that the probable cause of the USAir Flight 427 accident was the loss of control of the airplane resulting from movement of the rudder surface to its blowdown limit. The rudder surface most likely deflected in a direction opposite to that commanded by the pilots." The Board went on to specifically blame the power control servo valve: a big step in the right direction that put meteorological events in the rearview mirror.

At the time of the crash, the flight was being vectored by Pittsburgh Approach Control to land on Runway 28R at Pittsburgh International Airport. Their last assignment from ATC was a left turn to a heading of 100 degrees, a descent to 6,000 feet, and to maintain an airspeed of 190 knots. Visual flight conditions existed at the time. The airplane was essentially entering a downwind leg for the assigned runway 28R.

The first officer had just completed a routine public announcement thanking passengers for riding USAir and informing flight attendants to prepare for landing. "...certainly, appreciate you choosing USAir for your travel needs this evening, hope you've enjoyed the flight," he said. Those would be among the last words he would ever utter.

The plane was coming out of a left bank to wings level when it encountered some minor wake turbulence from another aircraft in the area. It is normal to use some rudder input in a turbulence encounter. But it appears that it was this use of rudder that caused the servo valve to mis-port and send the rudder to its blowdown position.

In an instant, the USAir 737 rolled severely to the left, driven by the errant rudder, which couldn't be countered by the ailerons—the primary roll flight control. One can tell looking at the roll trace from the flight data recorder that the pilot was trying desperately to counter the roll to the left with the ailerons.

At this point, the ATC blurts out, "USAir 427, maintain 6,000, over!" Seconds later, he hears shouting, "Pull! Pull! Pull!" and about three seconds later, the plane flew nose down into the ground at around 300 mph.

Flight 427 crashed into a wooded hilly area about six miles from the airport in a town called Aliquippa, Pennsylvania. No one survived. The crash site was so bad it was declared a biohazard, and the investigators on scene needed to wear biohazard suits. The cleanup required nearly two thousand body bags.

As to 737 fatal crashes, I now had in my head the following: Copa Airlines in Panama, China Southern, United 585 in Colorado Springs, and now USAir 427 in Pittsburgh. In addition, several incidences of pilots experiencing rudder hard-overs in flight had occurred where the flight crew had sufficient speed and a configuration to recover had been reported. Also, other pilots had experienced the rudder problem during preflight inspection. I learned from the mock-up in our hangar that there were more than twenty possible faults that could cause the rudder to misbehave. This wasn't just a one-off incident. The problem was prevalent.

United 585 and USAir 427 now seemed linked and it looked like the NTSB could no longer ignore the obvious.

For the time being, it looked like we knew more about the 737 rudder problem than anyone. Or, was it that no one else would admit it? By that I mean Boeing, the NTSB, and the FAA. These entities were the ones that could have corrected the problem and saved lives, but they moved too slowly and refused to admit the obvious. All three had exculpated the servo valve, claiming that the internal slides didn't have scratches or marks, which seemed to prove that this part wasn't the culprit. However, I could have shown them on a real unit how the servo valve could fail. But I knew they didn't want to listen. After all, I was a plaintiff's lawyer.

There was a picture of me in *Newsweek* magazine holding up a Parker-Hannifin servo valve, a device about the size of a juice can. The caption read, "**This is a holy war,** Colorado lawyer, Richard Schaden believes he has found the culprit in the crash of USAir 427." I explained to the *Newsweek* reporter what the problem was and how I didn't buy the official explanation about the need to have telltale marks such as scratches or gulling on the valve slides to prove that it was the culprit. I had strong proof otherwise. "This is the troublesome part, the servo valve," I said. "Some problems are like the icicle murder, they are deadly, but leave little or no evidence."

The reporter seemed to like that line. It helps that it was true. Now that the fact behind many of these crashes was out in the media, I was hoping it would be difficult to sweep it under the rug.

As previously stated, the Board did, in fact, reinvestigate the Flight 585 crash, rewriting and adding considerably more content to the original report and admitting the trouble with the servo valve. The extensively updated 585 report was issued March 2001. Unfortunately, before the updated report was released, I got involved in yet another 737 fatal crash that looked like the rudder was a contributing cause.

On December 19, 1997, Silk Air Flight 185, a B737-300, en route from Jakarta to Singapore crashed, killing 104 passengers and crew. Although our firm was not involved as lawyers, we were asked by the plaintiff's attorney to provide some technical assistance. We connected them with the expert witnesses that we had used in our 737 cases and gave them the empirical data from our 737 rudder test rig.

This suit was filed in California Superior State Court in Los Angeles against Parker Hannifin, manufacturer of the 737 rudder power control servo valve. Although there was a great deal of controversy as to the jury's verdict, the plaintiff prevailed. The United States sent an NTSB investigator to assist the local foreign investigators. In this case also, as was the pattern among the defenses came a claim that the captain had committed suicide.

The truth is, yes, there was a problem with the 737's servo valve. However, the real problem was the basic airplane design which forced so much tail power in the first place. The minimum acceptable fix would have been to split the rudder into two panels, each being powered by a separate and redundant system. But it was not likely to ever happen to Boeing's flagship 737 aircraft. The cost and optics would not let it.

In these later years, especially since Boeing has acquired McDonnell Douglas, I've been concerned about the Boeing culture without any real competition in the United States.

Clearly, Boeing has a monopoly in the United States when it comes to building airliners, but this wasn't always true. When I graduated from aeronautical engineering school, there were several manufacturers of transport-category jet airliners just in the United States. These included Convair, McDonnell Douglas, Lockheed, and Boeing. What happened to antitrust?

The worst-case scenario of my concerns regarding Boeing's special status in the United States would fully come to light in 2018 with the first crash of Boeing's latest 737, known as the MAX.

CHAPTER 15

The Boeing MAX and Longitudinal Stability

Where profit is, loss is hidden near by.

—*Japanese proverb*

Something's Wrong with the Piper Cheyenne

Sometime in the late 1980s, I was evaluating a potential product liability case involving the fatal crash of a general aviation twin-engine airplane, known as the Piper Cheyenne. Most of you will remember the Piper Cub, same company. It was my regular practice to find an airplane of the same model as that involved in the case, with a serial number as close as possible for the purpose of getting myself familiar with the product, and often to do some testing and/or analysis. This would help prepare me for expert witness preparation and cross-examination of defendants' experts at trial. Additionally, I would often instrument the plane to collect flight test data for design evaluation.

I found a Piper Cheyenne in Fort Wayne, Indiana, with a serial number very close to the subject airplane. I contacted the owner in an attempt to lease the plane for some flight tests and evaluation of the longitudinal flight control system, specifically the "stability augmentation system" (SAS).

We worked out a deal under which I would be required to take his pilot/mechanic along when I flew. We would be flying out of Fort Wayne International Airport (KFWA), where the owner was based. This was the first time I met Vern Gallmeyer, who turned out to be an exceptional pilot and airframe and power plant mechanic.

I explained to Vern that we would simulate a precision "approach to landing and a go around" at an altitude of 6,000 feet as indicated on the altimeter. I planned this high-altitude approach in the event the airplane would go out of control, which I was confident it would. This would give us plenty of altitude to recover. As I have said before, there is nothing so useless in an emergency as altitude above you.

I had arranged the weight and balance of the Cheyenne to be heavy and with the center of gravity (CG) as far aft as allowed by the flight manual. Vern was flying the approach to the imaginary runway in the sky. The plane was fully configured to land. The landing gear was down and full flaps were extended. At the pretend missed approach altitude, I called for a go-around, meaning that we were not going to land on the simulated runway for some reason, such as there was a cow on the runway. He added full power and started to retract the flaps. As he started to pull up, the nose went up rapidly, higher and faster than he intended. This pitch up was due to the change in longitudinal stability caused by the new, higher horsepower and much lighter engines of this model of the Piper Cheyenne. Next, the SAS (stability augmentation system) pitched the nose down rapidly, and he pulled up to correct, and again the SAS pushed the nose down. He and the stability augmentation system were in a tug-of-war. The plane was porpoising out of control. It took more than a thousand feet to recover—a luxury we wouldn't have had if this had been a real approach to an airport with hard terra firma.

Now Vern looked as shocked as he could be. He knew these airplanes well, and he was also somewhat of a Piper guy: he flew the planes, knew the models and preferred them to other aircraft brands. So, his reaction to the Cheyenne's behavior shocked him. When we got on the ground, I asked how he liked this kind of work.

It was obvious that he enjoyed it.

"You want to come work for me?"

He did and we then worked together for thirty years. Our friendship and working life grew from then on.

The longitudinal balance is usually one of the first steps in an airplane design project. The weight of every item of the aircraft, the lift of every airplane surface, the thrust of the power plant, and the airplane drag must be properly balanced. If not designed properly, the plane can become longitudinally unstable both statically and dynamically. Piper had been building a twin-engine, cabin-class airplane for years, known as the Navajo. But in the 1970s, they decided to follow their competitors and replace the piston engines with turbo-props. They chose the Pratt-Whitney PT-6, which as a pair put out around 1,200 horsepower. This was close to double the horsepower of the Navajo piston engines and also had a substantially better power-to-weight ratio, but they also shifted the center of gravity of the engines. These newly powered airplanes were called the Cheyenne and put Piper in the competitive league with Beechcraft, Cessna, and Aero Commander.

For an example of the industry trend, the Beechcraft Queen Air built in the late 1950s and early 1960s became the King Air outfitted with PT-6 turbo-props, which replaced the heavier lower-horsepower piston engines. This was an airplane that I had become quite familiar with since I had flown one owned by the Briggs family out of Detroit while I was in law school.

Cessna put turbo-prop engines on their cabin-class twin, and it became the Conquest. Aero Commander did the same to theirs, which became the Turbo-Commander.

Manufacturers have had a tendency of changing aircraft to remain competitive, but if you start changing a plane's engine thrust, weight, lift, or drag, you are flirting with longitudinal stability issues, which is what happened to the Cheyenne and as you will also see happened to the Boeing 737 MAX.

During the design process, one of the first tasks of any engineering team is to create a good control stick feel. That is, for the pilot to feel an increasing pulling force when pitching up and slowing and an increasing pushing force when pitching down and building up airspeed from a trimmed flight condition. Preferably, the stick forces should change linearly. In order to accomplish this on the Cheyenne, Piper installed what was referred to as a bob-weight added to the pitch control mechanism.

In my mind, the SAS system and the bob-weight were band-aids pasted on the Navajo. The Cheyenne should have been a new design on a clean sheet of paper, basically starting from scratch.

I flew the Beechcraft King Air quite a bit more than the Piper Cheyenne but had begun to hear Cheyenne stories dating back to the time it was first certified. In fact, Piper did have some problem getting some models of the Cheyenne to pass FAA certification. It seems that they barely snuck by the longitudinal stability requirement of the Federal Air Regulations.

I was first contacted by an estate lawyer to look into the crash of a Cheyenne in Germany. The plane had gone out of control climbing out of an airport on the edge of Munich, crashing into a McDonald's hamburger franchise, killing those in the airplane and killing and injuring several people on the ground.

It was a complex case from a legal perspective because of "conflicts of law" and the legal doctrine of "forum non conveniens." These are the kind of legal issues that we had become pretty good at since we can't get airplanes to crash in one forum or jurisdiction. It is very common to have the plane crash in a foreign country, the crew and passengers from another state or country, and the airplane or engine manufactured in a third jurisdiction.

But legal issues aside, I decided to learn the aerodynamic and stability and control details that plagued the Cheyenne. Ergo, Fort Wayne, Indiana, and Vern Gallmeyer.

I was involved in another Cheyenne case where six people were killed in a crash that occurred on an approach to runway 27R at Pontiac, Michigan. The plane was owned by a preacher who died in the crash. The weather was bad that day, and the pilot had descended to the minimum allowable altitude, didn't see the field, and decided to execute a missed approach similar to what Vern and I did in our test at Fort Wayne at six thousand feet.

The landing gear was down, and he was configured with full flaps. As he added full power, reduced flaps to the takeoff position, and retracted the landing gear, the plane suddenly pitched way up and nearly did a loop. The SAS system then pitched the nose way down as controlled by the angle-of-attack sensor signaling the SAS system. Because it was so close to the ground, the result was a horrible crash.

Stick pushers were a Band-Aid fix that have been added to a handful of airplane designs when they were unable to pass the aerodynamic stall warning and recovery requirement for certification by the FAA. I dealt with these issues in cases involving the Piper Cheyenne and the Learjet. Such problems came back to my mind when I first heard that Boeing's 737 MAX had gone down in Indonesia, followed by a second crash in Ethiopia within five months.

Boeing and High-Bypass Turbofans

All this talk of longitudinal stability and airplane reengining makes a good starting point to introduce Boeing's 737 MAX. The 737 itself is a platform that in my view has been long overdue for a blank-slate redesign rather than the tinkering it's been getting since the 1960s. It's no secret that I was never a fan of the B737, a topic that I've gone into detail at length in previous chapters.

In short, as an aeronautical engineer back in the 1960s, we were technically smarter from a viewpoint of safety, performance, stability and control, and flyability. A company like Boeing clearly could have done a lot better. Yet the B737 became the best-selling and most flown airliner in the world. I can only conclude that it was economics, branding, and chasing competition that sold this machine.

Training is also an issue that drives airlines to stay with a type and model. Simulators and other training issues are an identifiable operational expense for airlines. Thus, there is big economic motive to stick with a make and model as long as possible.

Obviously, the 737 can fly. But to me, it represents a balancing act of design trade-offs, stemming from the branding decision to hang the engines out on the wings (which required a massive and disproportionally powerful rudder), followed by many other economic decisions such as using only one rudder panel as compared to two, which likely would have saved the airplanes that fell victim to the hydraulic rudder hard-overs. Yes, it can fly from point A to point B. Most commuters will have flown on a 737 at least once, though probably several times in their lives. But the original geometric architecture, coupled with the subsequent decisions to fix the resulting problem, caused a recurrent balancing act between economics and good aeronautical engineering. The continued attempt to tame some of the ugly tendencies and noncompetitive performance of the 737 resulted in components that themselves had unintended consequences. The most recent of these classical problematic components on the Boeing Max is a system the corporation called the Maneuvering Characteristics Augmentation System (MCAS). Mostly, the MCAS was needed to deal with a stability problem caused by adding bigger, more powerful engines to the 737 in order to compete with the Airbus performance. Chasing the performance of a competitor by continuing to modify a design that is over fifty years old was questionable to start with and is doing substantial damage to the only real airliner manufacturer in the United States.

So, in December of 2010, when Airbus, Boeing's major competitor, announced the anticipated release of the A320neo family of aircraft, outfitted with a choice of the CFM International LEAP or the Pratt and Whitney PW1000G engines, touted to nil maintenance cost with 15 to 20 percent better fuel efficiency over the previous model, Boeing needed, or at least felt they needed, to come up with an answer.

But in June of that same year, Boeing had scrapped plans to totally redesign a new 737 from a blank slate to be certified with a new type certificate. They had just done that with the Dreamliner.

The Boeing 787 made its first flight October 2009, but it cost a great deal and had incurred some bad press during its early flights stemming from lithium-ion battery fires.

Whatever the thought process behind the decision, or what factors that lay behind it, with Airbus promising an upgraded, reengined, and improved A320, Boeing could not allow itself to sit pat. The decision was made again to keep the current 737 design but to give it bigger, more efficient engines.

As said, the newly minted A320neo came with two engine options, both of which gained efficiency by having higher bypass engines.

Turbojet engines achieve their thrust from the reaction to the jet exhaust that comes out of the tailpipe (for every action, there is an equal and opposite reaction). Turbofan engines achieve thrust from both a fan in the front of the engine and the jet exhaust. The fan is basically a multibladed ducted propeller that propels the air around the core of the jet engine. The bypass ratio is the ratio of the propulsion created by the fan as compared to the jet exhaust.

Especially at lower altitudes where more fuel is burned, the fan is the more efficient way to create thrust. That is why high-bypass-ratio engines have become so desirable.

Although these high-bypass-ratio engines are more efficient and powerful, they have continued to grow in diameter as the bypass ratio increases. The original JT8D engines on the Boeing 737 as certified in the 1960s had a bypass ratio of about 1.5 to 1. The MAX engine is about 12 to 1 and was much bigger in diameter.

If Boeing were to hang the more efficient and more powerful engines under the wing of the 737, something had to give because they were too big to fit. But they were going to make it work, and without a new type certificate, which would have cost a lot of time and money.

To do so, they pulled the engines forward on the wing, raised them so that the top of the nacelle (the casing covering the engine) was slightly higher than the wing leading edge, and canted them up. But this placement changed the balance of the major forces (thrust, drag, lift, and weight) on the airplane to the extent that both the static and dynamic longitudinal stability were substantially compromised. A fair reading of the Federal Air Regulations for the design of transport category airplanes would require any reasonable person to conclude that the MAX should have been on a new type certificate.

Maybe even a greater safety issue was pilot training and access to information. The pilots didn't receive proper information, nor were they properly trained with regard to the questionable band-aid fixes added to deal with the longitudinal instability, i.e., the MCAS and angle-of-attack sensors. The MAX was not the same plane as the NG (Next Generation, the 737 model just before the MAX). The differences were not negligible, but Boeing wanted to sell the MAX to the airlines as though they were basically the NGs while also touting the fact that the pilots would not have to be retrained.

The primary problem was that the MAX now had longitudinal stability problems, somewhat similar to the Piper Cheyenne. It didn't have an acceptable control force gradient and had a tendency to pitch up rapidly at high angles of attack in certain configurations. Just as in a Cheyenne, the MAX tried to fix the problems with a stability augmentation system that Boeing called the Maneuvering Characteristics Augmentation System (MCAS). One of the things that this system does is push the nose of the plane down if the thrust causes a rapid unintended pitch up at high angles of attack (AOA).

The pilots were neither properly informed about this device, nor were they trained on what to do when it was activated by an erroneous AOA sensor. Also, contrary to the requirements of the Federal Air Regulations, which required no "single point failure" that could cause a loss of airworthiness, this configuration should not have been certified.

Lion Air Flight 610

The reason that Boeing added this MCAS system wasn't as simple as Boeing wanted people to believe.

For starters, the MAX was represented to be just another upgrade of the 737NG (Next Generation). But in reality, it was a big change and needed a big fix. However, in order to avoid the expense of more pilot training, possible modification of simulators, and the possibility of a new pilot type rating, engineers added the MCAS to the flight control computers on a stealth basis to act in the background.

Unfortunately, neither Boeing nor their selected employees acting on behalf of the FAA under the Organization Designation Authorization (ODA) program investigated the dangers of the MCAS system in face of an erroneous AOA sensor. The AOA sensor provided the signal upon which the system relied. While there were two AOA sensors, one on each side of the nose of the fuselage, there was no redundancy and no "disagree indication" or protection. Although there were AOA indicators and "disagree alerts" on the 737NG, on the MAX, these safety devices were an option that were not on the Lion Air 610 airplane. The MCAS receives input from only one sensor during each flight. The left and right sensors alternate between flights, feeding angle-of-attack data to the MCAS feature of the Flight Control Computer (FCC). So, on one flight, you could have a good sensor available to talk to the MCAS and FCC. On the next flight, you might have a defective AOA sensor providing erroneous information to the FCC and its MCAS system. This happened to the fatal Lion Air 610!

On the day before the fatal flight, a defective AOA sensor was installed on the left side of the nose of the subject airplane. That afternoon, a crew, different from the accident crew, flew the accident airplane from Denpasar to Jakarta using Flight Number LN1043. On this flight, the crew had some issues, which included pitch control, indicated airspeed, and indicated altitude. Also of great significance, the left side defective AOA sensor caused the stick shaker to wrongfully activate throughout the flight and the MCAS system to repeatedly push the nose of the airplane down. Each time the nose went down, the captain would use pitch trim to raise it back up. The crew finally used the "stabilizer trim cut out switches" on the center console to end the tug-of-war. The passengers had a bit of a scary ride, but they arrived in Jakarta safely. Upon landing, the crew squawked some of the systems. The mechanics flushed the airspeed system, cleaned some electrical connectors on the "elevator feel computer," and cleared this 737 MAX as safe to fly. Apparently, the defective AOA sensor and the stick shaker were ignored.

The next day, October 29, 2018, the same airplane operating as Lion Air Flight 610 was cleared for takeoff on runway 25L from Soekarno-Hatta International Airport at Jakarta with 189 passengers aboard. Their destination was Depati Amir Airport, Pangkal Pinang City, Bangka Belitung Islands Province, Indonesia. They were in the air less than twelve minutes before crashing into the Java Sea and killing everyone onboard.

The maintenance issues on this airplane the day before concerning indicated airspeed, indicated altitude, and pitch control issues, should have tipped off the mechanics to examine the angle-of-attack (AOA) sensors. As the story of this tragedy unfolds, you will see that the bad left-side AOA sensor was the culprit. Also, it will become clear that the bad AOA sensor was a "single point failure," which should not have been allowed under the design standards for "transport category" aircraft as set forth in the United States Code of Federal Regulations, cited as 14 CFR Part 25. Under this regulatory law, the aircraft manufacturer was required to demonstrate by test, analysis, or both that failure of a system like the AOA sensor would be extremely improbable or in the alternative have the system backed up. Facts would support that the MAX was not in compliance in this regard.

As Flight 610 was taxiing onto runway 25L at Jakarta on the fateful morning, the captain sitting in the left seat was the pilot flying. The first officer, sitting in the right seat, was monitoring, making standard calls, and communicating on the radio. What neither pilot knew was that the AOA sensor on the left side was bad. It was providing the flight control computer and the MCAS system erroneous data of slightly more than twenty degrees. We know this from the black box (the digital flight data recorder) recovered from the sea. Had this MAX been fitted with the option for an "AOA indicator" and "AOA disagree," the crew would likely have aborted the takeoff. Less than 20 percent of the MAXs had this option. The AOA sensor on the right side, which wasn't in play for this flight, was working correctly.

As the captain advanced the power levers, both engines spooled up to takeoff thrust. Upon reaching eighty knots of speed, the first officer made the standard "eighty knots" call, indicating no problems up to that point. There would be only a couple of seconds to call out any problems. The next call was V_1, which meant that they were going flying even if there was a problem because they could not stop after this speed. There would not be enough runway left. After V_1, the crew would have to sort the problems out in the air and possibly make an emergency landing. This is one of the reasons redundancy and backup systems are part of the design requirements for transport-category airplanes. There should be no "single point of failure" that could render the airplane un-airworthy.

The next standard call was V_r, or rotate. The first officer called "rotate." As the captain pulled back on the yoke, the airplane rotated and the nose wheel lifted off the runway. At the same time, the "stick shaker" started. (The purpose of this shaker is to warn the pilot that the airplane is approaching an aerodynamic stall.) It should not have happened at this time. The plane was clearly above "stall speed." Not good! The "black box" would later show that the stick shaker continued through the remainder of the flight.

The airplane was now in the air and climbing, but additional problems were piling up. Within a minute or two, the first officer called "indicated airspeed disagree." This means that the indicated airspeed on the left side of the cockpit disagrees with that on the right side. Shortly thereafter, he calls, "Indicated altitude disagree." The crew didn't realize that the stick shaker, airspeed disagree, and altitude disagree alerts were symptoms of a faulty AOA sensor. These "alerts" were taking the crew's attention and causing confusion in the cockpit at a very critical phase of flight, and they were, in fact, facing a more serious problem, namely, their flight control computer and the MCAS system were being fed a bad signal by the AOA sensor. Later we would learn from the "black box" that the left AOA sensor was showing more than twenty degrees higher than the right AOA sensor, the right-side sensor being correct.

The air traffic controller, assuming everything was normal, cleared flight 610 to climb to their assigned cruising altitude of twenty-seven thousand feet or Flight Level 270. Within a few seconds, the controller saw that the aircraft was barely at one thousand feet and the crew was trying to determine their correct altitude compared to that indicated on the cockpit instruments. The first officer asked the captain if he wanted to return to the airport.

Just about then, the crew called for clearance to "some holding point" to sort things out. When the controller asked, "What's the problem?" the first officer responded, "Flight control problem." The captain then told the first officer to take over control of the plane while he troubleshoots the problems.

The plane managed to climb up to about five thousand feet over the next three minutes, which is a very slow rate of climb for a 737. All during this time, along with trying to respond to the various "alerts," the flying pilot had to deal with MCAS system pushing the nose down at regular intervals. Each time the MCAS would push the nose down, the pilot pulled back and trimmed the nose up. The MCAS would then push it back down. Also at this time, the plane was ascending and descending around the five-thousand-foot mark. All the while the pilots were fighting with the MCAS system to keep the airplane in the air, they were also reading checklists because of the flashing "alerts" and "disagree lights." In less than ten minutes, the MCAS won, and Flight 610 flew nose down almost vertically into the sea, while the MAX audio alert was screaming, "TERRAIN! TERRAIN!"

Boeing would later admit that the failure modes of erroneous MCAS activation, such as the defective AOA sensor, was neither simulated nor tested during validation tests to demonstrate compliance with the Federal Air Regulations.

Ethiopian Airlines Flight 302

As in the Lion Air Flight 610 crash, a defective AOA sensor also triggered the MCAS system on Ethiopian Airlines' practically new B737 MAX and caused a fatal crash on March 10, 2019, killing 157.

Flight 302 took off from runway 7R at Addis Ababa Bole International Airport bound for Nairobi, Kenya. It was a regularly scheduled international flight.

The Addis Ababa Airport is about 7,600 feet above sea level, and Flight 302 had a pretty good load. To the crew, this means that performance is somewhat impaired compared to taking off at sea level. But the crew had been trained for this type of operation. Airplane performance wasn't a significant issue, yet they were much closer to the ground while they were fighting with the MCAS system to save the airplane than the cockpit altimeters read since those instruments read altitude above sea level.

Just as the airplane rotated for takeoff, the left AOA sensor (vane) moved to an angle more than fifty degrees compared to the right sensor. This is an erroneous number that has no basis in reality. At this time, the stick shaker activated. Within one minute, the MCAS system pitched the nose down. Next, we hear "DON'T SINK" on the cockpit voice recorder (CVR, BLACK BOX). The pilot pulled back on the yoke and trimmed up with the electric trim switch on his control yoke. The plane leveled off for about thirty seconds. The captain yells, "Stab trim cutout," and the first officer hit the cutout switch. Again, the MCAS makes another nose down command, but the stabilizer doesn't move, apparently because the trim motor was out of the circuit now. The plane is now being hand-flown and has only a manual trim wheel on the side of the center console to trim the force out of the pitch control. Use of this trim wheel becomes very difficult or may be impossible. The captain yells again, "Pull up! Pull up!" The digital flight data recorder shows that both pilots were pulling hard. The MCAS had trimmed the stabilizer so nose down that both crew working together couldn't pull hard enough to save the 149 passengers, the cabin crew, and themselves. They lost the tug-of-war with the MCAS system just as the Lion Air crew did. The plane stayed in the air only about six minutes before it went nose down at a high speed into the ground.

As long as an erroneous signal is given by the AOA sensor and the electric trim motor is operative, the MCAS will continue to give incremental nose down commands. In response, the horizontal stabilizer trim will drive the airplane nose down. A human can quickly become exhausted, continuously trying to pull back on the yoke. If the trim motor is disabled after the nose has been driven down several times before the "trim cutout" is activated, it is very difficult to manually trim out the very large resultant forces. This is because the MCAS had the ability to drive the horizontal stabilizer to the full airplane nose down position.

Pilots were not told about the complexity of the MCAS system. They were led to believe that the airplane would fly like the B737 NG. The pilots were also led to believe that the flight control computer would follow the same laws.

Mechanically, the MAX was quite different, especially in the pitch axis. The placement of the higher-thrust, high-bypass engines had substantially changed the balance of the forces, which determine how the airplane flies. Boeing believed that it wasn't necessary to inform the pilots flying the MAX as long as the company could artificially make the flight controls feel like the B737NG by using digital electronic G-Wizz, officially called computer logic. They also had never properly tested the result of a failed AOA sensor.

Power, Lies, and the ODA

Two fatal crashes in five months for a brand-new cutting-edge aircraft is more than a disaster on many levels. Boeing is the marquee name in American aviation. It also happens to be the only name in the United States that still manufactures commercial airliners, making it a monopoly. Together with Airbus in the European Union, who increasingly sell their airplanes in the American market, they constitute a duopoly. What has happened to our free market and the benefits of competition as a means of checks and balances of trade in the United States and beyond? It seems as though antitrust is becoming a thing of the past. Look at Google, Amazon, Apple, etc.

I am not an expert in antitrust by any means, yet when it comes to Boeing, it seems that because they are a major exporter contributing to the balance of trade on a dollar basis in the United States, at least in the Pacific Rim, that the trust busters leave them alone.

When I graduated from aeronautical engineering school, there were several manufacturers of commercial airliners in this country. This created a healthy competitive environment. Now Boeing is the only game in town.

The federal government also used to care about preventing monopolies in the aviation industry. For instance, years ago, when North American Aviation, manufacturer of the Sabreliner, an executive jet, sought to purchase the Jet Commander, another corporate jet, the antitrust people stopped the merger. As a result, the Jet Commander was sold to an Israeli company and became the Westwind. But by 1997, we were down to only two manufacturers of commercial airliners, namely, McDonnell Douglas and Boeing, and the trust busters allowed the merger. And then there was one.

Did the merger lead to the 737MAX?

We can't say with precision. But it did lead to a corporation that faced no domestic competition and was in a real way linked to the United States government through its massive Boeing Defense, Space & Security Division (BDS). This is a group that touts themselves as the world's second-largest defense company. Furthermore, the corporation's position in helping the U.S. maintain its balance of trade, especially in the Pacific Rim, gives the company a special status and connection to Washington. Additionally, they have spent over fifteen million dollars a year in lobbying efforts.

Boeing's position as the United States' flagship manufacturer of jet airliner is why the story of the MAX is so shocking and at the same time predictable. It's shocking to discover that this iconic American company would put the sales of its new airplane above the lives of hundreds of passengers. But that is what happened. The company sold the airlines and the FAA a cock-and-bull story regarding the MAX and its similarity to the 737 NG and stuck to it at all cost. The pleading of a recent lawsuit by Southwest Airlines Pilots Association (SWAPA) puts it this way, "Boeing was specifically marketing the 737 MAX based on the 737 family's long track record for safety without disclosing the safety critical changes that made the MAX a fundamentally different aircraft from the prior generations of the 737 family." While the duplicity of this corporation is almost hard to believe based on the consequences, they were risking both in the number of lives lost and what that would mean to their stock price. Their behavior is also somewhat predictable considering their earlier history, especially regarding how they dealt with the 737's rudder problems.

When Boeing's only real competition entered the 737's market sector with an airplane that was much stronger in performance and cost of operation, Boeing found themselves in a tight spot. With their back to the wall and crunched for time, Boeing hung a state-of-the-art engine, one used by their competitor, on the most recent version of the 737, an airframe that was designed over fifty years ago, and the result was an airplane with competitive performance numbers and marginal stability and control. This was an upgrade that would also likely not have been found in compliance with the Federal Air Regulations, if not for the company's delegated authority to act on behalf of the FAA.

Judging by the transcripts delivered to Congress, Boeing employees and test pilots working on the project didn't view the plane too highly either. Several of the conversations in the transcripts would show employees were dubious about a pilot's ability to safely fly the airplane after MAX simulator training. Articles in both the *New York Times* and *Seattle Times* talk about misrepresentations made to the FAA about the operation of the longitudinal trim system operated by the MCAS. In fact, Boeing represented that the MCAS could only move the stabilizer 0.6 degrees, when in fact it could move it 2.5 degrees. This meant much greater airplane nose down, a fact that Boeing would later admit.

As the lawsuit filed on behalf of the Southwest Airlines Pilot Association (SWAPA) stated, "Boeing abandoned sound design and engineering practices, withheld critical safety information from regulators and deliberately mislead its customers, pilots, and the public about the true scope of design changes to the 737 MAX." Put in more succinct product liability legal jargon, "The 737 MAX was defective in design and the defendant manufacturer failed to instruct, warn and/or inform the buyers and users of the product as required."

The fraud and duplicity shown by this icon of American corporations would be shocking, if it wasn't already evident that the more powerful corporations get, the more arrogant they also get.

Boeing must be taken to task for what it has done and not done. On the other hand, the FAA should not be left off the hook, and it starts at the top. The Trump administration, from its first day, began to push for deregulation. Just days after his inauguration, President Trump signed Executive Order 13771 stating that, "For every one new regulation issued, at least two prior regulations be identified for elimination." A little over a month later, on February 24, 2017, another EO followed, this one titled, "Enforcing the Regulatory Reform Agenda," which states, "EO 13777 establishes the policy of the United States to alleviate unnecessary regulatory burdens placed on the American People; requires each agency head to designate a Regulatory Reform Officer responsible for overseeing the implementation of regulatory reform initiatives and policies." The second order is the means by which the previous order, 13771, would be executed.

All this is to say that at the moment the FAA was in the final stages of approving the MAX, Trump was putting the screws to federal regulatory agencies, including the FAA, and burdening them to drastically reduce regulations.

At the same time Boeing was pushing hard to get the MAX onto the market and our new president was signing executive orders aimed at cutting regulations across the board, the FAA would pass on one of the most dangerous airplanes in commercial aviation history, a plane that the FAA would later conclude, after the Lion Air crash, would have gone on to suffer one crash about every two to three years worldwide.

In previous cases against Cessna, I had put Mr. Obed Wells on the stand. Mr. Wells was a DMCR (designated manufacturer certification representative). He was a management employee of the Cessna Airplane Company but worked on behalf of the FAA passing on the airworthiness of Cessna airplanes. In fact, for several years, he actually signed the "airworthiness certificates" for each airplane that was delivered. He would take off his Cessna hat and put on his FAA hat and sign. To the jury, it looked like the fox had been assigned to watch over the henhouse. But by the time that Boeing had begun to certify the MAX, a new regulatory scheme had been initiated. Beginning under the Bush administration, a similar type of regulatory framework had been developed known as the ODA (the Organization Designation Authorization) program, which would allow certain company employees to act on behalf of the FAA and approve certain parts, or systems, of their employer's products.

As was the case when I was a young engineer at Boeing, the FAA neither had the funding nor the technical expertise to understand and pass on certain products or systems. This came to mean that the FAA had to rely on certain company employees to understand and regulate some of their own products. As time went on and automation and flight management system became more complicated, like the MCAS system, and the FAA had chronic funding problems, the agency began to rely even more heavily on in-house designated representatives.

While this situation may not have been the best of all scenarios, it is not expected that a company with the prestige of Boeing would systematically deceive regulators to bring a new plane to market. Doing so risks lives. If Boeing wasn't in a monopoly position in the United States and integral to its international economic position, lying to regulators, airlines, and pilots to maintain market share at the risk of human life should mean the death of a brand. It should certainly mean the regulators and maybe the antitrust folks take a hard look at this company.

Epilogue

Is tort law, including product liability and negligence, a good counterbalancing influence on the aircraft industry and the regulatory agency, namely the Federal Aviation Administration (FAA)? Is a check and balance system necessary?

Having investigated and litigated hundreds of airplane crash cases, I can say without hesitation, law has saved many, many lives. Tort law is a good and necessary check and balance on aviation safety.

There is a body of thought that the FAA is, and should be, the ultimate regulator of airplane design and manufacturing, and should not be second-guessed by tort law. In law, this concept is encapsulated in the doctrine of "Federal Preemption." Generally, that means, if the FAA has certified the aircraft or its components, a court or jury should not be allowed to find to the contrary. Here are some fallacies of the federal preemption approach:

- The FAA does not have the ability to maintain the same level expertise in many technical disciplines as does the private sector. Therefore, they are not totally qualified to regulate.
- The FAA is directed by federal statute to play a dual role, that is to both regulate and promote aviation, thus creating a level of conflict of interest.

- The FAA delegates employees of the aircraft industry to act on its behalf to pass on certification issues, thus creating yet another level of conflict of interest.
- The NTSB accident investigation team includes representatives of the manufacturers of the airframe, engines, avionics and other components who are inclined to protect their brand and their profits; and participate in writing the NTSB report including determining the probable cause of a crash.
- The NTSB investigative team doesn't include anyone to protect the interest of the pilots, passengers, or their families.

Tort cases have, and will, cause airplane design improvements and the addition of new life saving devices. The work of private accident reconstructionist, the debate of expert witnesses and university professors, and the development of demonstrative evidence have been a valuable check and balance on the aviation industry.

As we have seen time and time again over the last half century, left to their own, the aviation manufacturing industry will not automatically implement the necessary safety measures voluntarily, nor will the U.S. government hold them accountable. Therefore, work still needs to be done to put pressure on the airplane manufacturing industry to continue this effort. The concept of aviation design and engineering through law has proven to be much more effective than pushing for change from within the engineering departments of the manufacturers. The crusade must continue.